Start painting
pottery & bisque

Start painting
pottery & bisque

Scott Blades
&
Steven Jenkins

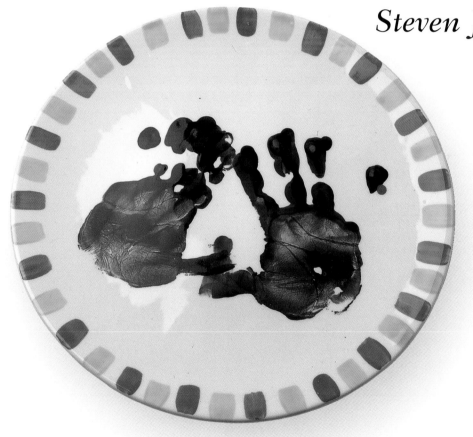

CHARTWELL
BOOKS, INC.

A QUARTO BOOK

Published by Chartwell Books
A Division of Book Sales, Inc.
114 Northfield Avenue, Edison
New Jersey 08837

This edition produced for sale in the U.S.A.,
its territories and dependencies only.

THIS BOOK WAS DESIGNED AND PRODUCED BY
QUARTO PUBLISHING PLC
THE OLD BREWERY
6 BLUNDELL STREET
LONDON N7 9BH

SENIOR EDITOR ANNA WATSON
TEXT EDITORS ALISON WORMLEIGHTON, AMANDA CROOK
MANAGING ART EDITOR FRANCIS CAWLEY
DESIGNER VICKI JAMES
PHOTOGRAPHERS PAUL FORRESTER, COLIN BOWLING
ILLUSTRATORS JENNIE DOOGE, SALLY CUTTLER
PICTURE RESEARCHER GILL METCALFE
PUBLISHER MARION HASSON
ART DIRECTOR MOIRA CLINCH

OPPOSITE: at your local firing studio
plaster molds are used to make
bisque items ready for you to paint.

PAGE 1: a hand-painted, zebra-stripe
tile by Georgina Noble.

PAGE 3: hand stamps by Adam Blades
on a bisque plate.

Manufactured in Singapore by Eray Scan Pte Ltd
Printed in China by Leefung Asco Printers Ltd

ISBN 0-7858-0941-4

contents

OPPOSITE: once the shaped item is removed from its mold, it is cleaned up, left to dry, and fired to make a bisque item for you paint.

How often have you thought how nice it would be to decorate your own ceramics? With the emergence of ceramic decorating studios, specially set up to cater for the individual, this is now possible. There is no need to invest in equipment or spend months testing various products—all the technical work, such as glazing and firing, is done by the studio, leaving you to enjoy the art of painting. Your first creation can range from being an absolute artistic disaster, to a masterpiece of world acclaim. Whatever the case, it's an original ceramic piece—one which you have created.

Ceramic painting can bring many pleasures. You will experience the enjoyment of working with your hands, and nurturing the creative side of your personality. You will have the joy of creating your own unique masterpieces, and friends will be delighted if you present them with a personalized ceramic gift which shows your thought and effort. The relaxing nature of ceramic painting, as you focus on the creation taking shape before your eyes, is one of its main attractions.

We focus on bisque decorating because it is an increasingly popular way of producing permanent ceramics, but you could also use the designs for decorating with on-glaze acrylic paints. Of course, it is possible to buy all the equipment and learn to produce handmade ceramics at home. However, this is both time consuming and expensive, and most beginners would be advised to use one of the many established studios. Here you can become familiar with the products used and the processes involved and, as you learn to select the relevant materials and techniques to produce the desired result, you have the chance to explore your own creativity. If you are interested, you can then investigate the more technical aspects of ceramic painting later on.

This book aims to provide you with the basic skills in underglaze decoration. Starting with a preformed piece of bisque, you can use the many types of underglaze colors available. The Basic Techniques section shows you different ways of applying color onto the bisque. The core of the book is the Decorative Painting Projects section, which contains 35 projects in many different styles and for a variety of bisque shapes. Individual projects can be copied directly with templates or adapted to suit your own designs or taste. The Gallery section displays other artists' work to encourage you to create your own unique designs.

By introducing you to the basic ceramic decorating techniques—eliminating most of the technical aspects and concentrating on the art of decoration—we hope you will be inspired to many hours of creative ceramic painting.

1 GREEN ITEMS. These are formed by pouring a wet mixture of clay called slip into a plaster mold. The slip sets on the inside of the mold, forming a shape that is removed when still wet and dried to form the greenware (raw clay) item. You can paint and sgraffito on greenware but it is very fragile.

2 BISQUEWARE (BISQUE) ITEMS. Once the greenware item is dry, the marks from the mold are cleaned off and it is fired. This produces a bisqueware (bisque) item, which is less breakable than greenware. Bisqueware is also sometimes known as biscuitware.

3 CLEAR GLAZE. Used to give the finished item a durable surface. Your studio will apply the glaze to a bisque item after you have painted it and then fire it in a kiln to give the item a permanent finish.

Design Equipment

You will get the best results in the ceramics studio if you have planned your design in advance. Here is some of the equipment which you may find useful.

1 STAMPS. These can be bought ready-made and are ideal for producing designs which repeat.

2 SPONGE SHAPES. You can buy these or make your own, and they are used for giving a repeated image with a distinctive texture.

6 MATT KNIFE. Used for cutting stencils or sponge shapes.

7 SCISSORS. You will need these for cutting tracing paper and carbon paper.

3 TRACING PAPER. Used to transfer your design from a template or other source onto the bisque shape.

5 CARBON (GRAPHITE) PAPER. Place the graphite paper face-down onto the bisque, and place a drawing or tracing on top. Trace around the design to transfer it through onto the bisque.

4 STENCILS. Again, it is your choice whether you buy pre-cut stencils or make your own. They are ideal for producing a shape with a sharp outline.

8 LEAD (GRAPHITE) PENCILS. Can be used directly onto greenware or bisque surfaces to set out a design. You can remove any unwanted marks using a standard eraser. if you don't get it right first time. The graphite is burnt off during kiln firing.

9 NOTE PAD AND DRAWING PAPER. Keep notes and sketches to help in reproducing a design or inspiration for further creations. Take notes of the colors and number of coats used.

Decorating Equipment

Your firing studio will provide all the equipment you need for decorating, but it is useful to know what your choices are before you start.

2 UNDERGLAZE COLORS. The main medium used for painting the design onto the surface, prior to glazing. A wide range of products is available, all with their own features. The main difference to be aware of is that some colors—usually dark or intense ones—need only one coat and can only be used on small areas. General underglaze colors need two or three coats to get a solid color, but can be used over large areas.

1 UNDERGLAZE PENCILS. Used to draw onto bisque or unfired color, these pencils give a textured line which looks like chalk on a chalk board. They will not burn off in the kiln.

3 BRUSHES. A range of general decorating brushes is used: fan and flat brushes for applying large amounts of color as evenly as possible, round brushes for general design, and designer brushes for long lines and small detail.

4 STYLUS TOOL. Incises into the color to reveal the bisque or an underlying layer of color. Ideal for detailed work.

5 SGRAFFITO TOOL. Incises into the color to reveal the bisque or an underlying layer of color. Ideal for bold lines.

6 FETTLING TOOL. Cleans rough edges from greenware and removes unwanted underglaze color. Used to remove mask by lifting up one edge enough so that you can grab the whole of it with your fingers.

7 DECORATING WHEEL. Used to support a bisque item so that you can turn it without smudging the paint. Also very useful if you want to paint stripes round an item.

8 SANDING BLOCK. One side is a foam sponge, the other an abrasive pad. Used to remove underglaze or graphite marks from greenware or bisque. Also ideal for cutting to produce sponged shapes.

9 MASK AND WAX-RESIST solutions. Used to protect an area of your design while the rest is being painted. Mask is removed prior to firing. Wax burns off naturally during the firing process.

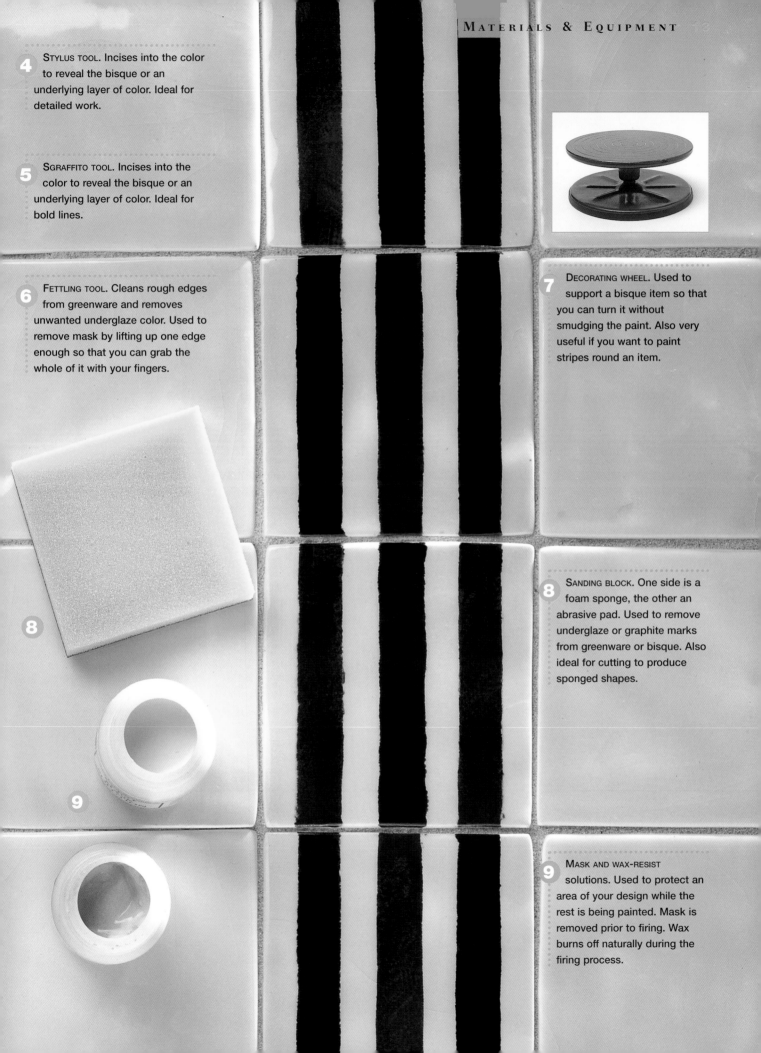

Basic Techniques

BRUSHES AND BRUSH STROKES

The size and type of brushes you use will have a tremendous bearing on the style and quality of your finished work. The old adage that a bad workman blames his tools is not strictly true in this case. A poor-quality brush can hinder the finest painter, just as poor-quality paint can affect a decorator. It is worth buying reasonably good brushes to begin with. A multipack of six brushes may cost a fraction of the price of two or three good durable brushes, but it is false economy to buy a range of sizes when you may only need two or three. Synthetic brushes today are as good as sable or squirrel—they keep their shape and last a reasonably long time. For a beginner a large, flat brush or fan brush, a ³⁄₈in- (1cm-) wide round brush, and a fine round brush with a good point should be enough to get you started, though you will soon need a few more.

1 FAN BRUSH

This is ideal for covering large areas or backgrounds. It can hold a fair amount of color and gives an even distribution. This is the best style of brush both for creating a watercolor-effect background and for applying repeated coats for a solid, even coverage.

After loading the brush with color you can produce a wide, solid line or an arc. The brush can be turned over to use the underglaze color forced through to the top side of the brush. Lifting the brush at the end of a stroke can give you a characterful "shaggy" effect. Petal-like curves can be worked by painting a part circle or shallow curve.

2 LARGE FLAT BRUSH

This is a good brush for covering a large area or for bold stripes and line work. Squares can be painted with short strokes. Finer, diagonal lines can be produced with the brush held at a 45-degree angle, to give a pleasing finish to a line. One coat of underglaze applied in random directions can give a background effect with great depth.

3 MEDIUM FLAT BRUSH

This brush is good for smaller areas of solid color or for graded effects (in which the brush is lifted gently off the bisqueware through the stroke). Used sideways, it can produce a bold line, as it will apply more color in a single stroke than a thinner, round brush.

4 ## LARGE ROUND BRUSH

This is an essential for the beginner, as it is ideal for a variety of brush strokes. A range of different effects and qualities of line can be achieved by raising and lowering the pressure of the brush against the ware. Pressing lightly and lifting off gently will give a fine line with a point. Pressing firmly and lifting straight off at the end of the line will give a thicker line with a rounded end.

5 ## MEDIUM ROUND BRUSH

Useful for obtaining petal, leaf, and floral shapes, this brush requires different amounts of pressure during each stroke. Begin with minimal pressure and increase toward the middle of the stroke, then decrease pressure until the brush is off the bisque. Alternatively, applying uniform pressure throughout a line will give a standard thickness. The angle of the brush against the bisque will change the thickness of the line— holding the brush upright gives a fine line, while holding it at a shallow angle to the bisque creates a thicker line.

6 ## FINE ROUND BRUSH

Perfect for fine detail and gentle outlines, this brush is also a wonder for touching in color on large areas or where a mask or stencil has left a gap. Varying pressure through a stroke produces great lines for flowing leaf and petal shapes. It can be used in conjunction with the other round brushes to build up a variety of linework. It is also ideal for crosshatching and shading.

7 ## SPONGE STICK

This is the ideal tool for putting a finishing line of color on the outside edge of a piece of work. It can also be used for banded lines or solid areas of color. Diamond shapes can be worked by pulling the tool at a 45-degree angle. Squares or solid lines can be painted by working with the tool held at a 90-degree angle to the bisque. Graduated lines can also be produced by applying curves, producing an unusual finish.

TRANSFER PAPER

Not everyone is a natural artist, but that need be no restriction here—you can simply transfer a design from paper onto the bisque. Draw your own design freehand on a piece of plain paper, which allows you to practice as much as necessary. Alternatively, trace an existing template from the Templates section. Once you have drawn the design, or traced it onto tracing paper, it is a simple process to transfer it to the ceramic surface using graphite or carbon paper. If you don't have graphite paper available you can use tracing paper to transfer the design across. In both cases the carbon from the graphite paper or from the pencil will burn off during the firing process, so it will not leave a visible mark on the finished item.

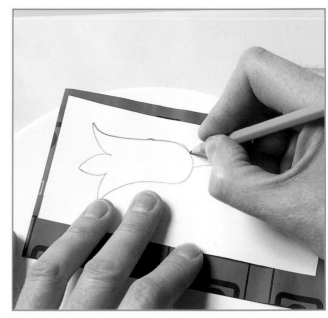

1 CUT AWAY ANY excess paper from around your drawing, to make it easier to position the design accurately on the ceramic item. Place a piece of graphite paper between the drawing and the bisque surface. Start to outline around the design, pressing firmly with the stylus or a pencil.

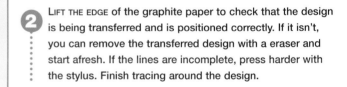

2 LIFT THE EDGE of the graphite paper to check that the design is being transferred and is positioned correctly. If it isn't, you can remove the transferred design with a eraser and start afresh. If the lines are incomplete, press harder with the stylus. Finish tracing around the design.

3 Remove the sketch and graphite paper to reveal the design—you can now select your color and begin to paint. Designs can be applied straight onto the bisque surface or on top of a base color. If using a base color, make sure it is completely dry or the pressure of the stylus may dig into the surface and leave an unwanted mark.

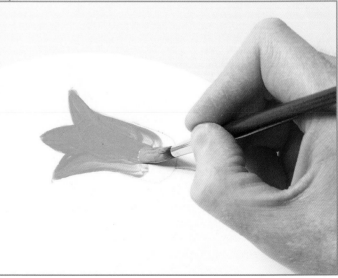

SPONGES AND STAMPS

Decorating bisque using sponges or stamps is a quick, fun way to apply simple designs. Sponging is not used to produce an accurate result but more to give the decorator a background to work on. Sponge shapes work particularly well on curved surfaces as they will bend to follow the surface contour. Bold, simple shapes are the most suitable for sponges, while stamps can be used for more detailed shapes. Ready-cut sponges and a variety of stamps are available from many specialist suppliers, or you can cut your own from sponge sanding blocks, which will give you an unlimited choice of shapes.

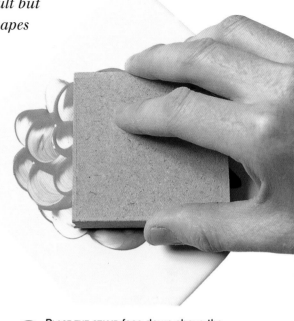

1 USING A GRAPHITE pencil, mark the position of each stamped image. Place a pool of color on a white glazed tile. Make sure you have enough color to coat the working face of the stamp. In this case a flower 2in (5cm) in diameter has a pool half this size. Be careful not to overload the stamp or you will lose detail.

2 PLACE THE STAMP face down above the pool of color so that the working surface just penetrates it. Move the stamp in a circular motion, spreading the color evenly across the tile and allowing the stamp to touch the surface as you do so. Lift the stamp and make sure the working surface is evenly coated with paint. Remove excess paint which may be trapped between any cut-outs (in this case the petals) with a brush.

3 APPLY THE STAMP to the surface to be decorated. Hold for a few seconds to allow the moisture to be absorbed, which will allow the color to transfer across. Be sure not to move the stamp sideways or you will smudge the design.

4 REMOVE THE STAMP. The color image has now been transferred to the ceramic surface. For additional images, place the stamp back in the pool of color and repeat the process. Add more color to the tile if needed.

SPONGE SHAPES

To make your own sponge shape to print from, cut out the desired shape from ⅜in- (1cm-) thick medium-density foam rubber, using scissors, a craft knife, or a mat knife. If the surface to be decorated is flat, the sponge can be attached to a piece of cardboard, which will help it maintain its shape. The sponge shape can now be loaded with paint and applied to the surface. Round or oval sponges can be used to produce very interesting paint effects. Sponge an entire area with one color then apply one or more other colors over the top. The result will be a mixture of all the colors. Use sponges with different textures for a wide variety of finishes.

1 PLACE A POOL of color on the tile. Gently press the sponge shape into the pool and work it up and down to allow the color to be evenly distributed across the working surface. Avoid pressing too hard as this would force the color up into the body of the sponge, reducing the amount that can be transferred to the bisque surface.

2 POSITION THE SPONGE above the ceramic piece, then gently push it down onto the surface. Make sure the entire working surface of the sponge comes into contact with the ceramic piece. If the surface is not flat, place one side of the loaded sponge on the surface and gently roll the sponge around the shape.

3 REMOVE THE SPONGE to reveal the transferred design. Repeat the process for further motifs. Any irregularities can be touched up with a smaller piece of sponge to maintain the mottled look.

HAND STAMPING

Many objects can be used to transfer a design onto your work, including leaves, textured material, even the sole of a shoe or a hand.

1 PLACE A POOL of color onto the tile and place your hand, or your child's, into the color. Slide it around the tile to evenly distribute the color over the palm and fingers and then lift the hand up, keeping it flat.

2 GENTLY PRESS THE hand onto the ceramic surface. Keep the fingers still and flat against the ceramic surface. Remove the hand, keeping the fingers straight to avoid disturbing the transferred color. Do not try to place the hand back onto the item to fill in any missing areas, as it is difficult to line up the prints. At this stage the transferred print will lack texture, but the textures will appear after it is glazed.

3 Paint a simple border around the design to finish it off. Hand stamping is very popular with children, so why not paint the child's name and age onto the item? This makes a fantastic momento of a child's growing years.

STENCILS

As with stamps and sponges, stencils are a fun, easy way to apply a design, though on ceramics they are generally used to set out the basic structure rather than producing the whole design. Once the color is applied through the stencil, additional detailing, by hand, will bring the design to life. The Child's Sheep Plate on page 64 is a good example of this approach. Precut stencils are available from craft centers, but making your own adds to the individuality of your work. Paper stencils are only suitable for limited use as the water from the underglaze colors will quickly render it unusable. Clear Mylar—the plastic sheets used for overhead projectors—can be used time and time again.

1 TRACE OR DRAW the outline of your design onto the stencil material. In this case we used a leaf shape. Cut out the leaf using a sharp craft knife or mat knife. Always cut toward you, holding the stencil with your free hand but keeping your hand out of the way of the knife. To change direction, turn the stencil, not the knife.

2 POUR A SMALL amount of underglaze color onto a tile. Pick up a clean, slightly moist sponge and dab one end into the color. Do not push too hard or the color will soak up into the body of the sponge. Dab the sponge about four times in the pool, to distribute the color evenly over the working area of the sponge.

3 PLACE THE STENCIL in the desired location, holding it down firmly. Sponge the color through the cut-out "windows" onto the bisque surface. Watch out for color running under the edge of the template. Apply as many coats as necessary to achieve the desired density of color.

4 CAREFULLY REMOVE THE template to reveal the neatly formed leaf. For a variegated leaf try using two colors. Stenciling leaves of different colors all over the surface of an item would produce a magnificent fall design.

5 USE A BRUSH to add some detail to the simple stenciled shape. Here we have outlined the leaf with dark green and added veins and a stem, making the stenciled shape come to life.

WAX RESIST AND LATEX MASK

The dilemma for all ceramic artists is, "How can I produce a colorful design with a solid background?" Most underglaze colors are semi-translucent, so one color applied over another will allow some of the underneath color to show through. This can be used to your advantage, but it is often undesirable. To paint around a design and achieve even coverage is very difficult as the colors need three coats for a solid, opaque finish. The solution is to use wax resist or latex mask.

Wax is used to protect a design while the background color is applied, then the wax burns off in a bisque firing. A latex mask is used to protect an undecorated area while the background color is applied, then the mask is removed leaving a clear area for the design. These products allow the artist to achieve a very even background in any color behind even the lightest design.

WAX SOLUTION

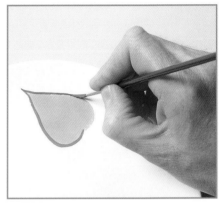

1 APPLY YOUR DESIGN using whichever technique you wish. Here a leaf was stenciled and the details painted by hand. It will be given an even yellow background using the wax method. Do not use your best brushes to apply the wax. During application, some of the wax will dry and stick to the hairs. Also, while cleaning there is always the likelihood of pulling out or breaking the hairs.

2 TO HELP STOP the wax from sticking to the hairs, condition the brush in liquid detergent (as used for washing dishes by hand). Wipe off the excess on a facial tissue. Now dip the brush into the liquid wax solution and apply one generous coat over your design. Be as neat as possible, as the wax edge will determine the outline of your design.

3 ALLOW THE WAX to dry, then brush the background color over and around the design. Apply enough coats for a solid coverage. Notice how the color on top of the wax forms small balls as it is repelled. Using a sponge or paper towel, remove these balls of color to stop them from transferring color through the wax during the firing process.

LATEX MASK SOLUTION

1 SKETCH OR TRACE your design onto the ceramic item using a graphite pencil. Condition the brush in liquid detergent as for the wax solution (step 2). As before, it is a good idea not to use your best brush, as it may get damaged. Apply one good coat of latex over the entire design, making sure that you leave no gaps within the shape which you want to be masked off.

2 Allow the mask to dry. Apply the background color as desired, painting directly over the masked area. In order to achieve the most even, opaque background, try to imagine that the mask is not even there.

3 THE MASK CAN be removed once the background color has lost its shiny, wet look. Slide the tip of the blade of a small knife or fettling tool under one edge of the mask. Lift the mask enough with the blade to enable you to grab it with your fingers.

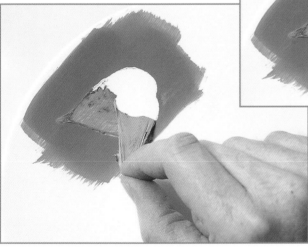

4 PULL THE MASK back over itself. It will come away in one piece leaving a clean area for application of your design. Run your finger around the outer edge of the design to remove any loose pieces of the background color. The edges can be neatened up using the curved end of the fettling tool.

5 Paint in the design as desired. In this case we have painted a white and green leaf on the royal blue background.

UNDERGLAZE PENCILS

Just as the thought of picking up a brush and painting with it can be quite scary, so the thought of having to apply writing or a fine line can be daunting. However, help is at hand. An underglaze pencil contains coloring oxide just like underglaze paints—it will not burn off in the kiln. The finished result has a slightly textured appearance, like chalk on a chalkboard. The pencils are only available in a limited range of dark colors (see Materials and Equipment section) and are not suitable for covering solid areas, so are only useful for linework.

1 Underglaze pencils are excellent for lining around the outside of your painted design. In the case of this sponged heart it helps to define the edge and strengthen the shape.

2 An underglaze pencil can also be applied on top of the underglaze color. Black lines on top of the heart give it a solid, three-dimensional look. It is important to allow the underglaze color to dry completely before attempting to draw on top.

SGRAFFITO

Sgraffito is a technique based on incising (scratching) through the painted colors into the surface of an item. Fine detail is easily achieved with either a stylus or a sgraffito tool, while larger areas can be scraped away using the sgraffito tool. The cleared areas can then be left as they are, with the bisque showing, or filled in with a color. The key to successful sgraffito work is to incise into the color while it is still a little damp. The tool will cut through it, leaving a neat, smooth line.

1 APPLY THE BASE color. Sgraffito works best through dark colors like black or dark blue—the bigger the contrast between the ceramic clay color and the underglaze, the bolder the finished design will look.

2 IT IS POSSIBLE to draw or trace your design onto the underglaze with a graphite pencil. Now use the stylus to incise around the design. Flakes of underglaze will form along the incised line, so brush these away with a dry soft-haired brush. If you find the underglaze is chipping and leaving a rough edge, use a damp sponge to gently sponge the area to be incised. Allow the water to soften the underglaze color and then continue.

3 THE SGRAFFITO TOOL is ideal for this technique, because a varying thickness of line can be achieved by angling the cutting edge. And it has a built-in brush, which can be used to brush away the flakes which form.

4 Continue until you have cut out all the outlines and any wider areas, such as the center of the flower. The sgraffito tool can be used for this too. Any color can now be applied directly onto the clay base—it will hold its true brightness. Additional areas, such as the petals, could also be scraped away and more colors inserted.

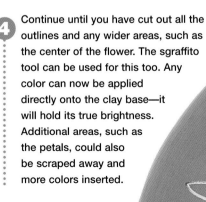

DESIGN INSPIRATIONS

Perhaps the most daunting thing about painting ceramics is being presented with a plain, white shape to decorate. Overcoming the fear of making any mark and "spoiling" the piece is the first hurdle. One thing in your favor is the lucky fact that all the pencil or carbon lines will magically burn away in the firing process so nobody will know how many attempts it took to get the finished version.

COLOR BASICS

For a beginner, even just learning about color can be fun. Many people will have painted a traditional color wheel at school without understanding fully how it worked. Primary colors—red, yellow, and blue—are the basis of all the colors we can see. Secondary colors are formed by mixing any two of the primaries, to give orange (from red plus yellow), green (from yellow plus blue), and purple (from red plus blue).

Tertiary colors can then be created by mixing a primary with a secondary to produce even more subtle shades, such as red-orange or yellow-green. Different tonal values are created by thinning the color or adding a little white for a pastel version, or by adding a little black to create a darker version—but be careful not to "muddy" it too much.

Many people have a tendency to automatically outline everything in black. However, selective or free outlining works better, as it adds more life and energy to a piece of work. If outlines are necessary, try using different colors that are more in keeping with the work. Pastels fade to nothing when outlined in black—a medium gray is kinder and does not affect the subtlety. Natural color ranges work better with a brown or warm-colored outline. Highly stylized or graphic images are often best with a clean, black outline. Think the design through first to make the right decision.

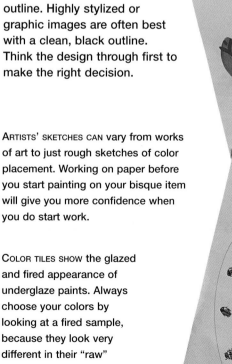

ARTISTS' SKETCHES CAN vary from works of art to just rough sketches of color placement. Working on paper before you start painting on your bisque item will give you more confidence when you do start work.

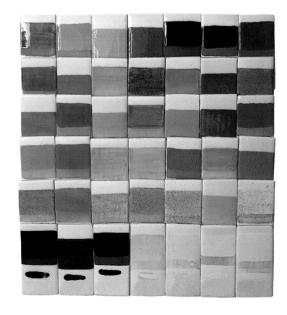

COLOR TILES SHOW the glazed and fired appearance of underglaze paints. Always choose your colors by looking at a fired sample, because they look very different in their "raw" unfired state.

Overlaying different bands of underglaze color will give you a good idea of the variety of colors you can create. Because the underglaze colors are like watercolors, you can see the undercoat through the top color. For example, painting yellow lines on a blue background should give you green, while red lines on blue will create purple. Some of the underglaze ranges, however, have very opaque colors, and dark green and some purples are so thick that they completely cover the color underneath.

A good way to get started decorating is to do your own color test. Apply one large brush stroke for each of your colors around the edge of a plate. Paint a second coat of the same color over half of the brush stroke and a third coat over half of that. You will then have an accurate reference guide to the depth and coverage of each of your colors. This can be invaluable, whether you are painting an area that has to be solid and flat, or you just need a subtle wash effect over an area.

Paintbrushes are not the only method of applying color to the bisque.

Anything that can carry color can be used—such as the end of a pencil, a sponge, a potato, or pieces of fabric. Paint can be flicked to give a spatter effect, dribbled and splashed in the style of Modern Art, or dragged and scraped in the way an interior decorator would use it.

Colors can be offset against each other and used to your advantage. For example, a mug painted blue with a red interior and an identically shaped mug with these colors reversed would look very different. This is because "warm" colors (reds, oranges, yellows) appear to advance, making them look closer or larger, while "cold" colors (blues, greens, purples) appear to recede, looking more distant or smaller. The mug with the red exterior would therefore appear larger than the blue one.

All these different factors will come into play when you are decorating your bisque item. You may be surprised at how much color sense you have already and how quickly you can put this knowledge to use.

DESIGN BASICS

Everyone has a basic appreciation of design from an early age. Whenever we choose one item over another, we are weighing up design at some level. Choosing a particular car or style of furniture requires some consideration of design. As regards the plain white item of bisque you have in front of you, there are a number of questions you can ask in order to start focusing on a potential design:

- What is its function?
- What room will it go in?
- Will the item have to blend in with its surroundings?
- Who will it be for?
- Are there elements you must include, such as a name or date?
- Does the shape restrict or dictate the method of decoration?

Once you have answered some of these questions, you will hopefully have narrowed down your choices and be nearer an end result. Sometimes, of course, it will be easy to decide on a design and you can get straight on with it, but often a little preparation is needed, especially if you are producing a gift or an item for a special occasion.

You may wish to start with a plain background color and see how the design develops. An all-over coat of yellow on a vase may help the piece to blend into, say, your family room or living room. Do you want to add a pattern, such as a botanical study, chintzy sprigs or a geometric motif? Perhaps texture is all that is required to add interest to the vase—for example, sponging on some ochre for a soft, subtle effect against the yellow, or black or red for a strong contrast. You may then decide to add random white lines to echo some Venetian blinds or louvered shutters in the room. Ideas often develop in the unlikeliest ways once you have started.

As well as deciding where to start, it is equally important to recognize when to stop. You may spend hours on a piece only to decide you preferred it halfway through. Don't feel you have to finish every stage of an idea just because you planned it that way—if your eye says it looks good and you don't need any more, stand back and pause for thought before continuing. You may decide it needs that finishing touch but equally you may think it's fine as it is and so put your brush down.

THE YELLOW OF the lemons repeated in the background gives a harmonious and integrated design. In contrast, putting a single pale flower against a dark background emphasizes its exotic shape.

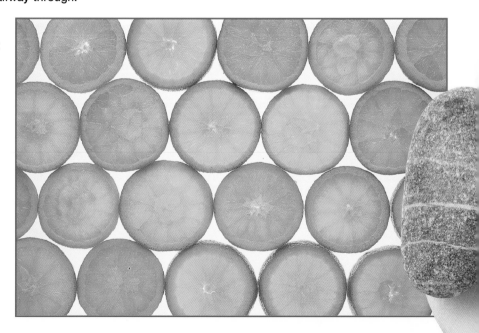

DON'T BE AFRAID to use simple patterns and strong colors. The effect of repeating orange slices could make a dramatic decoration for any bisque item with large, flat surfaces.

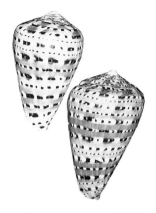

Another simple way of beginning a design is to look for the natural divisions in a piece. With a teapot, for example, you have a handle, body, spout, and lid. If each of these is done in a different color, whether contrasting or tonal, a pleasant design will be created and you will also start to think about the shape as you work with it. Moreover, the second time you decorate a teapot, you will have an idea about which areas are best (or easiest) to decorate and which will not be seen or do not merit detailed work. The idea could then be adapted to cups, saucers, sugar bowls, and milk jugs, using your original idea and changing the size or amount of detail or pattern to suit the shape and function of the item. A large flower might look fine on the side of a teapot but could look odd if used in the same scale on the side of a cup. Perhaps the design would look fine on a saucer and so the cup might only need to be painted in the same background color to make them match.

If you are not confident about your drawing ability, the design can be photocopied to the size required and transferred to the bisqueware with graphite paper. Tracing paper is also a boon for keeping an image accurate. Precut stencils can easily be adapted for ceramic work or you can make your own with sheets of Mylar. If you use the clear type, you can place the image exactly where you want it and see clearly around the edge of the design.

LOOKING CLOSELY AT objects can reveal design ideas, such as the striking, abstract patterns on these shells.

THE COLOR CONTRASTS in this mixed media collage could inspire you to decorate an item with turquoise underglaze paint and bronze luster.

REMEMBER THAT SIMILAR designs occur naturally at different sizes. A large shell motif can look good on a dinner plate, but could also be repeated at a smaller scale on other items. Pebbles have interesting textures that could inspire you to sponge color onto an item, rather than using a paintbrush.

DRAW ON YOUR favorite jewelry or fabric swatches for ideas on color and shape. The stencil pattern below was based on a traditional American quilt design.

FINDING INSPIRATION

Once you become involved in a craft such as pottery decoration, you start looking at everyday objects in a slightly different way. For example, you may decide to base a design on a postcard showing a beach or woodland view. One approach would be to draw the view and try to adapt this to the shape you would like to decorate. You may only need to add some extra sky for a tall item like a vase or to widen the view for a bowl or platter. An alternative approach is to pull the view to pieces and then reassemble the component parts. If you like the color of the sand or trees, say, a simple banded pattern could be worked with blue (sky), green (woodland), light green (foreground), and brown or black (for a baseline) to finish. Pattern could be added with squiggles to suggest the trees, white flecks for clouds, and a column of horizontal lines in brown to suggest tree trunks. Postcards are a cheap and plentiful source of inspiration and it is worth holding on to any that appeal, as you never know when you may need that extra detail to add to a project.

Other good sources of reference include magazines and periodicals, textiles, historic houses and architecture, natural history, botanical illustration, sport, cooking, and so on. Your style of decoration can reflect your interests. A good vacation or weekend trip can provide endless inspiration, and a quick sketch or photograph is an excellent starting point. Even a brief visit to a museum or gallery can send the imagination into overdrive.

You may find you veer toward a specific area of the decorative arts, a certain period in history, or the art of a particular culture or part of the world. Whether it is Ancient Egyptian mummy cases or Native American jewelry, there is so much decorative source material that you should never be short of ideas. Patterns from rugs and ikats are ideally suited to adaptation and their color palettes have been tried and tested over hundreds of years, so you can't go far wrong with them.

Keep a special notebook or folder for notes, cuttings, fabric swatches, wallpaper samples, leaves and flowers, and packaging. Everything you keep can help you acquire a designer's eye. A series of notebooks with different areas of interest could help if you are in search of a new theme or a change of style. You might have one for each of the following categories:

THE NATURAL WORLD

Photographs of plants, animals and rock formations provide plenty of ideas, and there is endless scope in the undersea world: fish, shells, the boundless formations of corals, and even the coloring of the reefs. The patterns and vivid colors of bird feathers and animal prints need little adaptation.

LANDSCAPE

The natural formations of the earth can be amazingly decorative. Coastal rock formations and pebbles are obvious sources of material. Cliff faces and snow-covered ranges have individual color and textural values.

ARCHITECTURE

Architecture offers an unbelievable wealth of inspiration. Tiles and mosaic floors from the Roman to the Victorian eras, stained glass and decorative window panels, colored brickwork and stone carving are all good sources.

STUDY THE WAYS that fabric designers have simplified natural forms into stylized shapes. The vase on the left uses simplified shapes to great effect— consider a trip to your local museum as an investment in inspiring design ideas.

DELPHINIUMS AND DAHLIAS combine strong colors with interesting shapes. Try to match the flower's shape to the proportions of the bisque item you want to decorate.

INTERIORS

Photographs of the interiors of historic homes and those of the rich and famous can make an interesting collection. Even if you don't use them directly, they are good as a launching pad for other ideas. Examine how designers have used ceramics, wallpapers, and furnishings in these interiors, how items have been put together, how patterns and styles are mixed. Although you may not like individual items in a room, you may still admire its overall look or its color scheme. The more information you have to choose from, the better.

LETTERING

It is always a good idea to keep any clippings of decorative lettering or calligraphy as these can be useful when dedicating a piece of work or personalizing something. Magazines, logos, and even bags from stores are good sources. Always sketch out your lettering first to get the spacing and placing correct.

CERAMICS

Finally, a scrapbook of other pieces of ceramics that you like can help when you are on the hunt for an idea. The way a potter or designer decorates a handle or even the backstamp on an Oriental pot can be reworked to suit your style and taste. There is really very little that cannot be used as a source for your work, as you will see from the projects we have prepared for you.

Decorative
Painting Projects

The 35 projects in this section of the book are illustrated with step-by-step photographs to show how they are painted. You will notice that the colors of the paints as they go onto the bisqueware are different from their final appearance when glazed and fired. You will always need to check your colors against a fired sample, which will be available at your local studio.

The projects include a range of different techniques and styles. Some are painted freehand but for others you will need to copy the design from the Templates section (pages 114–125). However you choose to work, and whichever patterns you choose to use, we hope that once you have mastered the basic techniques and built up your confidence, you will start to adapt the designs and create ceramic masterpieces in your own style.

Making a present for a child is one of the most rewarding aspects of painting your own ceramics. The enduring image of a duck is used to decorate this child's bowl. Soft, watery colors and rich yellow and orange combine to make a great pattern for you to present to your favorite small person. There is plenty of scope for personalizing or adapting your gift. A name could be added underneath or incorporated into the pattern of the bowl. You could change the color of the background or work a matching mug and plate for a full nursery set.

Sponged Ducks
Child's Bowl

Sharon Clark

YOU WILL NEED

BISQUEWARE bowl
UNDERGLAZE PAINTS IN COLORS LISTED BELOW
LARGE FAN BRUSH
SPONGE
PERMANENT MARKER
CRAFT KNIFE
TILE
LARGE ROUND BRUSH
FINE BRUSH

COLOR KEY

LIGHT BLUE

YELLOW

MEDIUM BLUE

ORANGE

BLACK

1 GENEROUSLY LOAD A LARGE fan brush, and paint the inside of the bowl in light blue, working with broad strokes. When this is dry apply a second and third coat and leave to dry. Paint the underneath if desired.

2 DRAW THE OUTLINE OF the duck on a sponge using a permanent marker (see Templates section). Holding the sanding block over a firm surface, use a craft knife to cut around the outline. To avoid cutting into the shape work in sections from the duck's shape outward.

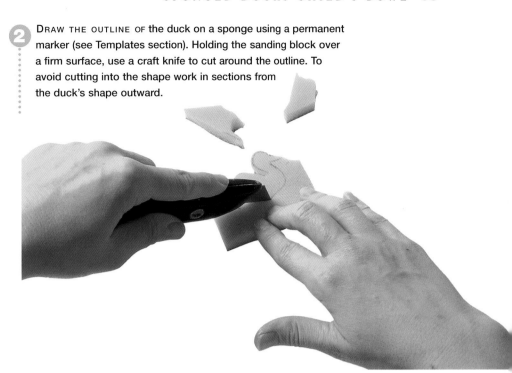

3 POUR SOME YELLOW UNDERGLAZE onto a tile and spread it out with a fan brush. Place the sponge flat on the paint and press down. Try sponging a duck onto some paper to get an idea of how much pressure you will need to exert. Reload the sponge and press it carefully onto the bowl, with the image level. Reload the sponge and add another duck on the opposite side. Apply two more ducks spaced equally between the first two. Only one coat of color is needed.

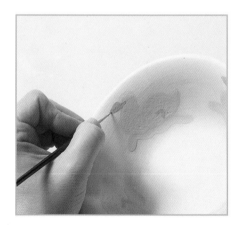

4 WITH A LARGE ROUND brush, paint a bold flowing line in medium blue under each duck, working from the front to the back. Press hard with the brush against the bisque at the beginning of the stroke, lifting off gently until you reach the end. This will give a neat finish to the stroke and help to suggest the water. With a fine brush, paint orange beaks and feet on each duck; you will need three coats here.

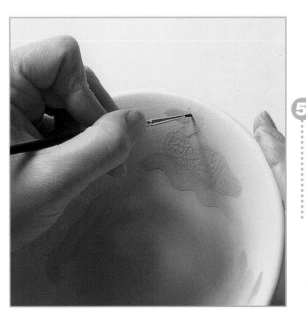

5 USE A FINE BRUSH to add black eyes, working them as dots and applying only one coat. You may want to draw them in pencil first to make sure they are well placed.

Plaid Plate

Sue Taylor

Plaids, checks, and stripes are never out of fashion. These eternally popular patterns lend themselves perfectly to plates, as the lines can be taken right up over the rims without interruption, and a dramatic effect can be produced in a short time. The lines are painted freehand so that they are slightly wobbly, giving the design more character. A set of these plates would look superb displayed on a hutch or hanging on a wall. You could even adapt the design to incorporate the colors and pattern of a particular tartan.

YOU WILL NEED

BISQUEWARE PLATE

UNDERGLAZE PAINTS IN COLORS LISTED BELOW

PENCIL

RULER

MEDIUM FLAT BRUSH

SMALL FLAT BRUSH

COLOR KEY

YELLOW

GREEN

1 USING A PENCIL AND ruler measure and mark out three equally spaced broad stripes across the plate and then three stripes the same width at right angles to them. Try to set the pattern slightly off-center as this will look better.

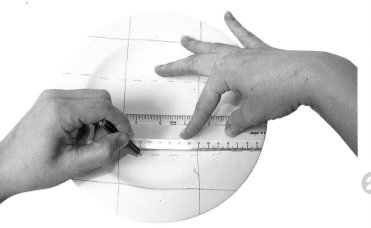

2 USING A MEDIUM FLAT brush, paint the yellow stripes in one direction. When dry, apply two more coats of yellow.

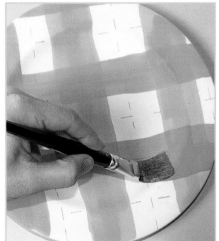

4 WORKING WITH A SMALL flat brush, paint green lines between the yellow stripes and outside the outer yellow stripes. When dry, apply two more coats of green.

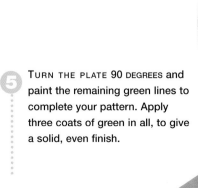

3 TURN THE PLATE 90 DEGREES and paint the yellow stripes in the other direction using the same brush. Once again, apply three coats in all. Where the stripes intersect, the color will be deeper.

5 TURN THE PLATE 90 DEGREES and paint the remaining green lines to complete your pattern. Apply three coats of green in all, to give a solid, even finish.

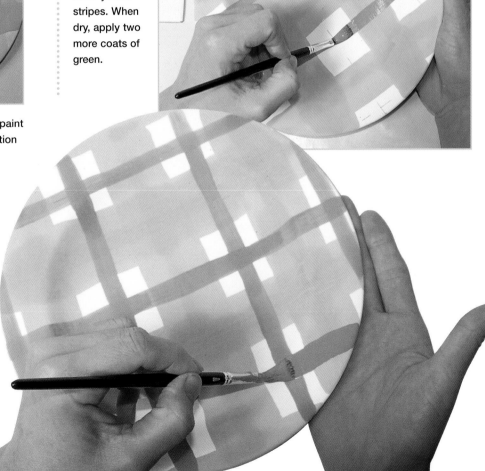

Cat's Bowl

Sue Taylor

This cartoon-style bowl is surely an encouragement for any cat to finish its meals. Decorated with fishbones, paw prints, and a cheeky ginger face, it is a project suitable for all ages. Simple to work, it should also be speedy to finish. Personalize the bowl for your own cat, or a friend's, by simply changing the coloring of the face; also, there is room to fit a name around the face or around the outside. In the template section we have also provided a template for a dog's face so that all your pets can have lovely food bowls.

YOU WILL NEED

BISQUEWARE BOWL

UNDERGLAZE PAINTS IN COLORS LISTED BELOW

PENCIL

TRACING PAPER

MEDIUM ROUND BRUSH

SMALL ROUND BRUSH

LARGE FAN BRUSH

COLOR KEY

ORANGE

BRIGHT GREEN

PINK

BLACK

2 WITH A MEDIUM round brush, paint the cat's face in orange, painting the outside of the shape first and then filling in the middle; do not paint the muzzle or the eyes. Use only one coat so that the color will appear pale and slightly textured with brushmarks.

3 PAINT ORANGE STRIPES on the cat's face using the same brush. (You may need to draw these out in pencil beforehand.) This second coat of color will show up as a stronger color on a pale orange background. With the same brush, apply three coats of bright green to the muzzle (except for the nose and tongue) and the eyes.

1 TRACE THE TEMPLATE from the Templates section onto some tracing paper. Transfer the design to the center of the bowl, making sure the positioning is correct. Draw alternating fishbones and paw prints around the outside edge of the bowl.

5 USING THE MEDIUM brush, apply three coats of orange to the paw prints around the outside of the bowl. With the small brush, paint the fish heads and tails around the outside with three coats of bright green. Use this brush to outline the paw prints in black. Do the same for the fish heads and tails, adding the bones as straight lines.

6 LOAD A LARGE FAN BRUSH well with orange, and lay it flat against the rim of the bowl, leaving a bar of color. Repeat three times at equal intervals. In between, paint four bright green bars using the same method.

4 WITH A SMALL brush, paint the nose and tongue with three coats of pink. Now, using the photograph as a guide, outline each area in black. Paint the pupils of the eyes and the whiskers with black too.

Ideal for a gift, this vase covered with roses and rosebuds will look as good empty as when it is brimful of fresh blooms. The 1950s-inspired design appears complex but is actually very simple to achieve, as the pattern builds up from basic shapes. The black background sets off the lilac and red of the roses beautifully but the design would also work well with pastel flowers against a blue or soft-colored background.

Rosebud Vase

Steven Jenkins

YOU WILL NEED

BISQUEWARE VASE

UNDERGLAZE PAINTS IN COLORS LISTED BELOW

PENCIL

LARGE ROUND BRUSH

MEDIUM ROUND BRUSH

SMALL ROUND BRUSH

FINE BRUSH

COLOR KEY

RED

DARK RED

LILAC

DARK LILAC

LIGHT GREEN

DARK GREEN

BLACK

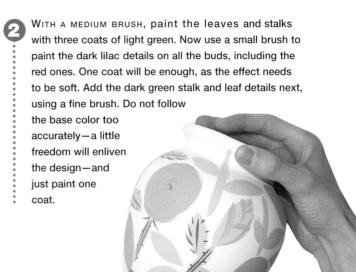

2 WITH A MEDIUM BRUSH, paint the leaves and stalks with three coats of light green. Now use a small brush to paint the dark lilac details on all the buds, including the red ones. One coat will be enough, as the effect needs to be soft. Add the dark green stalk and leaf details next, using a fine brush. Do not follow the base color too accurately—a little freedom will enliven the design—and just paint one coat.

1 DRAW CIRCLES OVER THE outside of the vase with a pencil, trying to space them fairly evenly. Draw leaf shapes between the circles and then lines to represent stalks between the leaves. The spacing is what is important at this stage, so draw only the outlines. With a large brush, paint the rose heads in swirling movements, using red and lilac alternately. Apply two or three coats of each color.

4 FILL IN THE BLACK background with a medium brush, leaving a little white showing around the edges of the flowers, leaves, and stems. Apply three coats of this color for a glossy finish.

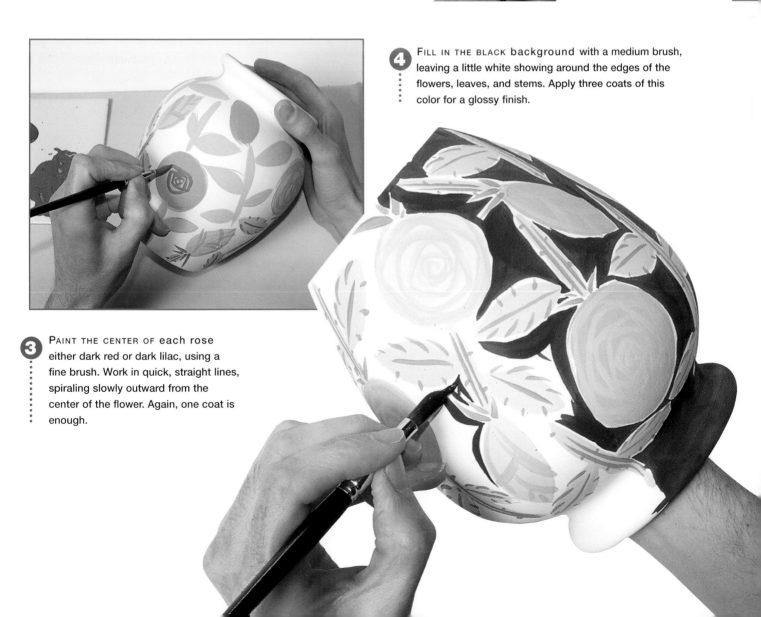

3 PAINT THE CENTER OF each rose either dark red or dark lilac, using a fine brush. Work in quick, straight lines, spiraling slowly outward from the center of the flower. Again, one coat is enough.

Wax Resist Fruit Bowl with Pears

Sarina de Majo

Stylish and modern, this bowl shows off its shape with a simple garland border. The stylized fruit motif is a clever mix of colors that combines the techniques of sponging and wax resist to good effect. A great opportunity to show off your own talents, it is an ideal gift for anyone with an interest in fine and applied arts, although it is also a piece you probably will not want to give away!

YOU WILL NEED

BISQUEWARE FRUIT BOWL

UNDERGLAZE PAINTS IN COLORS LISTED BELOW

PENCIL

MEDIUM ROUND BRUSH

SMALL SPONGE

DETERGENT

FACIAL TISSUE

WAX RESIST

LARGE FAN BRUSH

COLOR KEY

YELLOW

MEDIUM GREEN

LIGHT RED

ORANGE

BLACK

2 PAINT THE YELLOW garland border and the yellow pears with a medium round brush. On one side of each pear, paint a light coat of medium green using the same brush. Now use a small piece of sponge to speckle the border and pears with orange, pressing gently with only a little paint on the sponge. Lightly sponge the lower half of the border pattern in medium green, and a little of this color on the pears too.

1 DRAW THE BORDER pattern in pencil, building it up from simple curves. Draw the pear outlines inside the bowl on the bottom, keeping them similar in scale. Try not to make them too big, as the bowl needs a large area of black to attain the final effect.

3 WITH A CLEAN, dry piece of sponge, sponge small areas of the border pattern in light red, using the photograph as a guide. Also sponge a thin layer of light red over the pears, avoiding the right-hand side of each pear and applying a heavier layer to the bottom left-hand side of each to give a shadow effect.

4 WHEN THOROUGHLY DRY (sponged color can take longer), dip a medium brush in detergent and wipe off the excess on a facial tissue, leaving the brush fibers coated with a protective layer of detergent. Paint a solid, even coat of wax resist over the pears and the border pattern. Only the areas covered with wax will be seen on the finished work. Leave the wax to dry thoroughly and wash your brush immediately in detergent and hot water. The wax will burn off during the firing.

5 WITH A LARGE fan brush, paint the outside of the bowl with three even, solid coats of black, leaving it to dry between coats. Now paint the inside in the same way—the areas covered with the wax will resist the color and you will be able to see how the finished item will look.

Strawberry Cream Pitcher

Sharon Clark

Strawberries and cream are one of summer's indulgences, and this cream pitcher will remind you of picnics and alfresco meals on balmy days. Quick and easy to do, the pitcher is also very satisfying when put to use! A sponged background sets off the giant, ripe strawberries, which are designed so as to make an all-over pattern. A simple color range and the graphic representation of the fruit help to produce a fabulous design.

YOU WILL NEED

BISQUEWARE CREAM PITCHER

UNDERGLAZE PAINTS IN
COLORS LISTED BELOW

TILE

NATURAL SPONGE

PENCIL

CARD (OPTIONAL)

SMALL ROUND BRUSH

MEDIUM ROUND BRUSH

COLOR KEY

LIGHT RED

MEDIUM RED

GREEN

ONE-COAT WHITE

BLACK

1 POUR SOME LIGHT red underglaze onto a tile, and dip a small piece of natural sponge into it. Practice sponging on a tile or a waste piece of clay to check the amount of color and pressure you need to use. Press the loaded sponge against the body of the pitcher, lift it off, turn the sponge slightly, and press again in another patch. (Changing the direction of the sponge helps to stop a pattern forming.) Reload the sponge with color and apply another two or three patches. Continue in this way until you have an even coverage on the pitcher and the handle. Now sponge a thin coat of medium red all over the pitcher.

2 WHEN DRY, DRAW the strawberry shapes around the pitcher. You can make a card template to draw around (see Templates section). With a small brush, paint the stalks on each of the strawberries green. Three coats of color may be needed to cover the red background.

3 USING THE SAME brush, add the white seeds in rows, working from the top of each strawberry downward. Try to place them evenly and don't overfill the strawberries.

4 OUTLINE THE STRAWBERRIES in black using the small brush. Do the stalk first and then the outside, painting in a flowing, fine line. Take care not to smudge the black, as it could stain the white seeds. Finally, paint alternate black and green brush strokes around the top rim and spout of the pitcher, by holding a medium brush over the rim and painting outward.

Toothbrush Holder

Joe Crouch

Shells and starfish are wonderful reminders of childhood days or romantic vacations, and are among the most popular of all motifs on items ranging from intricate rococo mirrors to small, inexpensive souvenirs. We have used a free, modern approach with a loose, painterly style to create a charming toothbrush holder for the bathroom. Rich colors and flowing lines give this project a fun look that is easy to achieve. One coat of paint on the starfish and shells will give a translucent effect, while a second coat will create a richer, more opaque finish.

YOU WILL NEED

BISQUEWARE BEAKER

UNDERGLAZE PAINTS IN COLORS LISTED BELOW

PENCIL

MEDIUM ROUND BRUSH

SMALL ROUND BRUSH

FINE BRUSH

SMALL FLAT BRUSH

COLOR KEY

GOLDEN YELLOW

LIGHT ORANGE

PURPLE

LIGHT RED

DARK GREEN

LIGHT BLUE

BLACK

1 DRAW SIMPLE OUTLINES of the motifs on the beaker in pencil, tracing from the Templates section if you wish. Try to space out the motifs as evenly as possible and avoid placing two similar shapes next to each other.

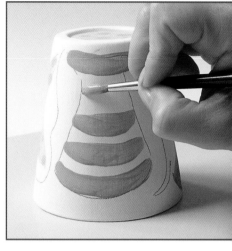

2 WITH A MEDIUM round brush, paint the base of the beaker and the starfish in golden yellow, painting the outside of the shape first and then filling in. When the paint is dry, use the same brush to paint spots all over the yellow areas in light orange, spacing them fairly evenly.

3 WITH THE SAME brush, paint a broad, slightly curved purple stripe at the bottom of the scallop shell. Now paint broad, curved purple stripes across the shell. You may want to mark these in pencil first; keep the gaps between stripes thinner than the actual stripes.

4 USING THE SAME brush, paint the top of the periwinkle light red in two curved strokes, and the rest with light red stripes, as for the scallop shell but using a small brush at the bottom to achieve a neat point. The dark green seaweed is painted next and can be placed anywhere in the design to fill a large space. Paint it with a couple of flicks of the medium brush to create a flowing effect.

5 ADD THE BACKGROUND in light blue, painting round the edges of the shapes first and then filling in. Leaving a small unpainted space here and there keeps the pattern lively. Also paint the inside of the beaker this color. One coat should be sufficient.

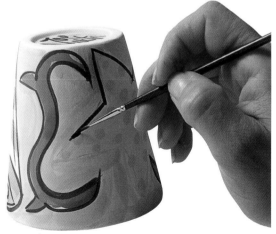

6 LOAD A FINE brush well with black underglaze and paint the outlines with swift strokes, varying the thickness of the lines here and there. Keeping rigidly to the paintwork is not necessary.

7 A DENTILED BORDER on the inside of the beaker adds a final touch. With a small flat brush, paint little strokes about an inch (2 or 3cm) deep from the inside upward, spacing them evenly. Finish off the rim running the brush round it to give a solid black line.

A favorite with children and adults alike, the ladybug is the least likely insect to make anyone retire in fright, and its markings make it a favorite with illustrators and designers. The central motif of the ladybug on a leaf could be transposed to almost any shape, and the others would make a great all-over pattern on a vase or other vertical piece.

Ladybug Plate

Silva Lee de Majo Burrows

YOU WILL NEED

BISQUEWARE PLATE

UNDERGLAZE PAINTS IN COLORS LISTED BELOW

PENCIL

FINE ROUND BRUSH

MEDIUM ROUND BRUSH

COLOR KEY

GREEN

RED

YELLOW

BLACK

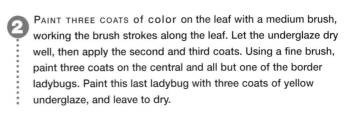

2 PAINT THREE COATS of color on the leaf with a medium brush, working the brush strokes along the leaf. Let the underglaze dry well, then apply the second and third coats. Using a fine brush, paint three coats on the central and all but one of the border ladybugs. Paint this last ladybug with three coats of yellow underglaze, and leave to dry.

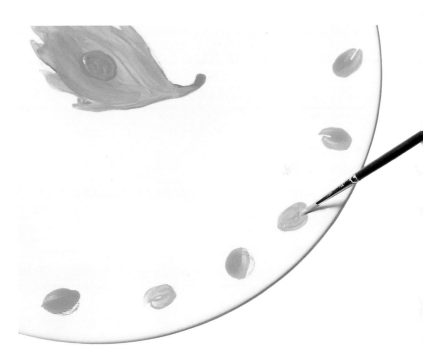

1 DRAW THE CENTRAL leaf motif and ladybug in pencil. Mark out appropriate-size circles around the edge of the plate; the details will be added later. Try to balance the spacing—avoid getting the ladybugs too close together, and remember that you need room to add the legs!

3 PAINT EACH OF the border ladybugs with a fine brush and some black underglaze, starting with the central line, then the outer wings, head, antennae, and finally three legs on each side. Add the spots, aiming to give each insect slightly different details. Draw the center stem and leaf veins in pencil, then paint them with the fine brush. Outline the leaf, and then paint the central ladybug in the same way as the border ones.

Carrot and Leek Mug

Sharon Clark

This lively mug is a perfect example of a pattern that is wholly suited to its shape. The alternating orange and green also add a sense of fun. Vegetable motifs have made a revival recently in interior fabrics and wallpapers, and they are bound to be popular for years to come. If you enjoy doing this design there will be no end to the variations of pattern and shape you can adapt from it. Almost any vegetable can be simplified into an outline, then all you need are a few appropriate brush strokes.

YOU WILL NEED

BISQUEWARE MUG

UNDERGLAZE PAINTS IN COLORS LISTED BELOW

PENCIL

WIDE FLAT BRUSH

MEDIUM ROUND BRUSH

FINE BRUSH

COLOR KEY

ORANGE

LIGHT GREEN

LIGHT RED

MEDIUM GREEN

BLACK

1 SKETCH (OR TRACE FROM the Templates section) the carrots and leeks onto the mug with a pencil. You may find it helps to draw lines ½in (1cm) in from the top and bottom of the mug to keep the motifs even. Paint orange stripes with a wide flat brush in the appropriate sections for the carrots. Then, working with the light green, paint a line over the leek shape, but only about two-thirds of the length. Lift the brush gradually as you finish the stroke, to capture the graduated coloring of the leeks.

2 USING A MEDIUM BRUSH, paint small horizontal strokes on the carrots in light red. Don't paint each stroke the full width of the carrot—just use short, light strokes to give a bit of texture. With the same brush and the medium green, paint down to the halfway mark on the leeks. This will create a gradual darkening toward the top of the mug.

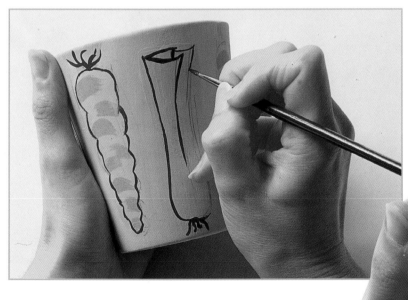

4 FINALLY, WITH THE MEDIUM brush, paint bars across the handle of the mug in orange, medium green and light green. It is important not to neglect areas like these, as they will make all the difference to a project's success.

3 WITH A FINE BRUSH, paint the outlines and detail on all the vegetables. The tops of the carrots are painted in black and the roots of the leeks in the medium green. You may need to redraw the details before you start painting the outlines.

Mosaic Planter

Ornella Galuccio

This planter is an ideal piece for a contemporary bathroom or living room. A broad range of ocean colors forms a background to the central motifs, mirror-image seahorses and a bright red heart. To create the mosaic effect, each square "tile" is painted separately, and the outline is scored to give a clear outline. The technique is best tried out on a smaller item first. Almost any motif could be adapted, with a grid placed over it—depending on the final use of the item, you could adapt the color range.

YOU WILL NEED

BISQUEWARE PLANTER

UNDERGLAZE PAINTS IN COLORS LISTED BELOW

PENCIL

GRAPHITE PAPER

FINE ROUND BRUSH

MEDIUM ROUND BRUSH

SGRAFFITO TOOL

COLOR KEY

RED

LIGHT RED

MEDIUM BLUE

CHARTREUSE GREEN

SAND

LIGHT ORANGE

DARK BROWN

DARK BLUE

LIGHT BLUE

LIGHT GREEN

2 DRAW THE GRID over the outside of the planter, making the "tiles" about ½in (1cm) square. Divide the motifs into slightly smaller squares, except for the seahorse spines—leave these undivided.

1 USING THE TEMPLATES provided, transfer the image of the seahorses onto the planter with graphite paper or by tracing. Draw the heart in the center, and work the wave pattern along the base of the planter, and a simple wavy line along the outer rim at the top.

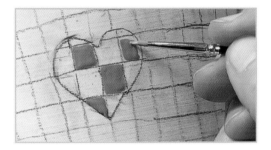

3 USING A FINE brush, paint three coats of red underglaze on alternate squares within the heart, then paint the remaining heart squares with a lighter red.

4 PAINT THREE COATS of medium blue on the wave area, and alternate "tiles" in alternate medium blue and chartreuse green on the top wavy line. Paint three coats of sand on the seahorse bodies, and three coats of light orange on the spines, using a medium-size brush. Use a fine brush to paint the seahorses' eyes in dark brown.

5 WORKING WITH A range of blues and greens, including medium blue and chartreuse green, paint all the squares that form the background three times, including the rim. Try to space the colors out fairly evenly and avoid having too many squares of one color together.

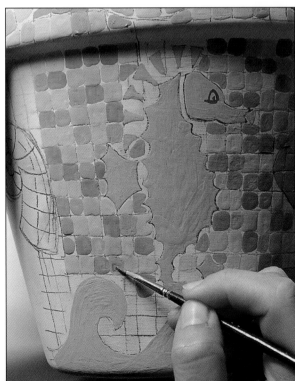

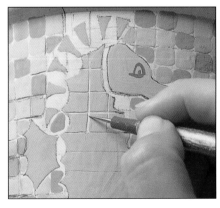

6 USING A STYLUS or sgraffito tool, score around the edges of each square. If you wish to avoid doing this all at the end, you may want to work some sgraffito areas as you progress. Brush off any dust to ensure that the final piece will be clean for firing.

This lively design brings botanical illustration right up to date. A range of greens loosely outlined in black is set against the natural color of the earthenware on this piece. The easy-to-draw motif is scattered over the body of the mug, while decorative stripes are applied to the handle and the rim is finished with an attractive band of brush strokes. An ideal gift for a gardener or anyone with green fingers, a set could be worked with different vegetables, or a mixture of motifs could be used on one larger item. Your kitchen could become a ceramic market garden!

Pea Pod Straight-Sided Mug

Sharon Clark

YOU WILL NEED

BISQUEWARE MUG

UNDERGLAZE PAINTS IN COLORS
LISTED BELOW

PENCIL

MEDIUM ROUND BRUSH

SMALL ROUND BRUSH

COLOR KEY

MEDIUM GREEN

CHARTREUSE OR LIME GREEN

BLACK

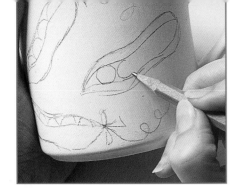

2 WITH A MEDIUM BRUSH, paint one even, solid coat of medium green on all the pods and on the stalks.

1 DRAW THE PEA PODS in pencil on the mug. (Refer to the Templates section if you need.) Try to get all the motifs at different angles and space them as equally as you can. This will stop the design from looking too stiff when finished. Once you have the basic spacing you can draw in the details such as the peas.

3 USING THE SAME BRUSH and the same color, paint the outside of the pods with a second coat to give them a darker tone. Likewise, paint the tops and bottoms on the half-opened pods and just the undersides on the others. This gives a shadow effect which helps the pods look three-dimensional, but do try to keep the edges of the pods fluid and neat.

4 THE NEXT STAGE IS to paint in the peas. You may need to pencil your guide lines in again before beginning. Give all the peas one good coat of chartreuse or lime green to make them stand out against the background color.

6 WITH A SMALL BRUSH, outline the pods and paint the details in black. Paint a thin line along the tendrils. A loose outline will suit the style of the design so don't worry if you go over the edge here and there.

7 USING THE PHOTOGRAPH AS reference, paint stripes down the handle in green and black alternately. A border of brush strokes worked along the rim is the perfect finishing touch; for the neatest finish here, work with the brush at an angle.

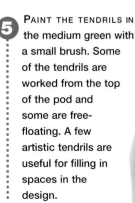

5 PAINT THE TENDRILS IN the medium green with a small brush. Some of the tendrils are worked from the top of the pod and some are free-floating. A few artistic tendrils are useful for filling in spaces in the design.

This elegant pitcher is decorated with a swimming figure set against a textured underwater background, and the fish adds a touch of humor to the piece. Ideal for lemonade on a hot summer day, this is a piece that is sure to impress. It is worked in easy steps and will also give you some practice with painting techniques. The figure would work equally well on a wall plaque or a platter and would make a striking impression in a bathroom or a beach house.

Swimmer's Pitcher

Sarina de Majo

YOU WILL NEED

BISQUEWARE JUG

UNDERGLAZE PAINTS IN COLORS LISTED BELOW

PENCIL

TRACING PAPER

CARBON PAPER

STYLUS (OPTIONAL)

MEDIUM ROUND BRUSH

FINE BRUSH

COLOR KEY

FLESH

LIGHT RED

MEDIUM BLUE

STRONG WHITE

YELLOW

DARK BLUE

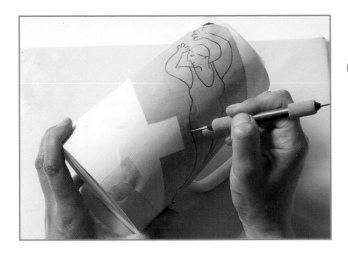

1 USING A PENCIL AND tracing paper, trace the template from the Templates section. Position the figure on the jug and then slip a sheet of carbon paper underneath. Redraw the figure with a pencil or stylus through the tracing and carbon paper. Remove the tracing and peel the carbon paper off. You may need to redraw the image in places.

2 WITH A MEDIUM ROUND brush, paint the skin in flesh color, applying three coats and allowing it to dry well between. With the same brush, paint the costume and cap in light red, again applying three coats. The toenails are applied in a single coat of light red.

3 USING THE SAME BRUSH, paint the sea in medium blue, making sure the brush has lots of color on it and reloading it frequently. Begin with the area around the figure and use small strokes in different directions. You may want to practice this on a tile beforehand.

4 LOAD A FINE BRUSH well and paint the petals on the costume in strong white, using single strokes from the center of the flower outward. Paint a flower on the cap, too. You could draw the outlines in pencil before you begin, but do not press too hard or you might lift some of the color.

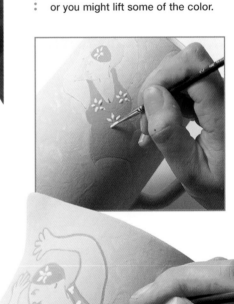

5 PAINT THE CENTER OF each flower as a yellow blob, still using the fine brush. Paint a small fish under the swimmer in yellow (drawing it in pencil first if necessary). Three coats will be needed to cover the blue. Give the fish red lips as an extra touch of fun.

6 THE FINAL STAGE IS to outline the figure in dark blue. With a fine brush, carefully work around the face and body, trying to keep the same thickness of line throughout. Outline the fish in the same color. It is worth practicing the outlines on a blank piece of bisque or some paper first.

Fruit Bowl with Lemons & Limes

Joe Crouch

Mouthwatering citrus motifs float freely all over this giant fruit bowl. As bright and modern as can be, this piece deserves pride of place in a kitchen or dining room. The lively style is quick and easy to work and is a great release if you have been working on a small, detailed project. With very little adaptation, it could be altered to suit a dinner service, or the motifs could be changed to apples and pears, or perhaps green and black grapes.

YOU WILL NEED

BISQUEWARE FRUIT BOWL

UNDERGLAZE PAINTS IN COLORS LISTED BELOW

PENCIL

LARGE ROUND BRUSH

MEDIUM ROUND BRUSH

FINE BRUSH

COLOR KEY

YELLOW

ORANGE

BRIGHT GREEN

DARK GREEN

LIGHT RED

BLACK

1 DRAW THE DESIGN in pencil, to be sure of the spacing. Copy the shape from the Templates section if you want to get the outline traced exactly. Use a large brush to paint both lemons and limes with one coat of yellow, using bold brush strokes and painting the outsides of the shapes before filling in. At each stage, paint the fruit on both the inside and the outside of the bowl to keep the color uniform. When the first coat is dry use the same brush to add an orange shadow to each lemon.

2 WITH THE SAME brush, paint the limes with a coat of bright green, on top of the yellow. Then paint bright green leaves between the fruits, again painting the outsides of the shapes first and then filling in. Draw simple leaf shapes around the rim of the bowl, spacing them evenly and keeping them roughly the same size. Paint these leaves bright green in the same way as the others.

3 WITH A MEDIUM brush, paint a dark green shadow line on each lime and bold dark green outlines on all the leaves. (Don't do this to the leaves on the rim until they are dry.)

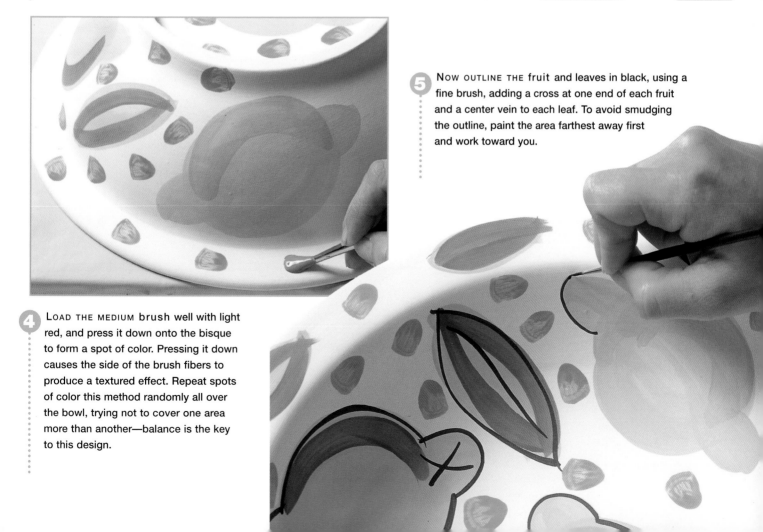

5 NOW OUTLINE THE fruit and leaves in black, using a fine brush, adding a cross at one end of each fruit and a center vein to each leaf. To avoid smudging the outline, paint the area farthest away first and work toward you.

4 LOAD THE MEDIUM brush well with light red, and press it down onto the bisque to form a spot of color. Pressing it down causes the side of the brush fibers to produce a textured effect. Repeat spots of color this method randomly all over the bowl, trying not to cover one area more than another—balance is the key to this design.

Art Nouveau Mug

We took the colors and decoration from the early twentieth century for this project. The finished design crosses the years quite neatly by using traditional colors on a modern shape. Soft swirls and organic forms keep the pattern fluid, while the brown outline is more in keeping with the period flavor than a harsh black would be. The design would work equally well on delicate coffee cups and saucers or on a large, flamboyant lamp base.

Steven Jenkins

YOU WILL NEED

BISQUEWARE MUG

UNDERGLAZE PAINTS IN COLORS LISTED BELOW

PENCIL

SMALL ROUND BRUSH

LARGE ROUND BRUSH

FINE BRUSH

SPONGE STICK

COLOR KEY

LILAC

PURPLE

TURQUOISE

LEAF GREEN

CHARTREUSE

MEDIUM BROWN

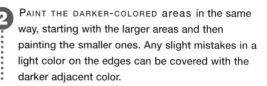

2 PAINT THE DARKER-COLORED areas in the same way, starting with the larger areas and then painting the smaller ones. Any slight mistakes in a light color on the edges can be covered with the darker adjacent color.

1 DRAW YOUR DESIGN ON the outside of the mug with a pencil, keeping all the lines as free-flowing as possible. Begin painting the larger light-colored areas, using a small brush to delineate each area and then a large brush to fill in. Paint the smaller light-colored areas next, using the small brush. Apply three coats for good coverage.

3 USE A FINE BRUSH to outline the blocks of color in medium brown. Start with the larger areas, leaving the fine detail to the end. Add a wavy brush stroke line down the handle.

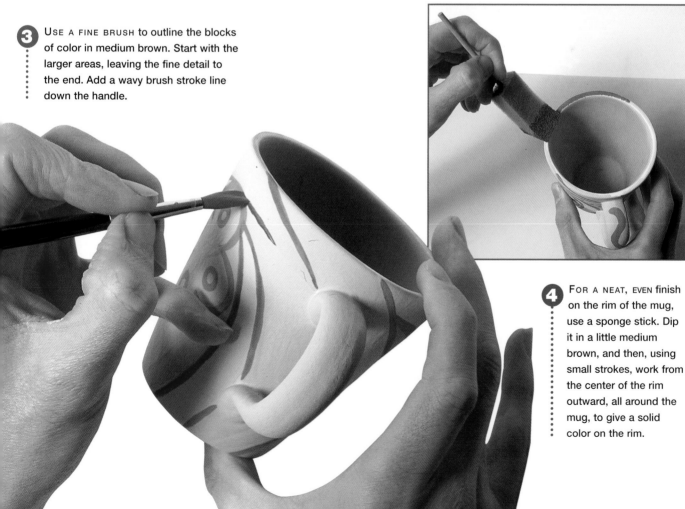

4 FOR A NEAT, EVEN finish on the rim of the mug, use a sponge stick. Dip it in a little medium brown, and then, using small strokes, work from the center of the rim outward, all around the mug, to give a solid color on the rim.

A teapot may look like a daunting shape to decorate, but as you can see, the secret is to be bold—and what could be bolder than these wild roses and leaves floating in complete freedom over the entire pot? This is an ideal style to emulate, as you will be able to adapt anything to the simple stages and bold, fluid outlines. The trick is to keep the brush loaded with color and not to worry if you go over edges. Worked in naturals or in fizzy, bright colors, this will sit well on any tea table or dresser.

Roses Teapot

Joe Crouch

YOU WILL NEED

BISQUEWARE TEAPOT

UNDERGLAZE PAINT IN COLORS LISTED BELOW

LARGE ROUND BRUSH

PENCIL (OPTIONAL)

MEDIUM ROUND BRUSH

FINE BRUSH

COLOR KEY

LAVENDER

SPRING GREEN

TURQUOISE

BLACK

1 WITH A LARGE BRUSH, paint bold circles in lavender on the body of the pot. Two or three on each side should do. Paint the outline first and then fill with color, working two coats in quick succession with a well-loaded brush. The circles and leaves can be drawn on first in pencil if you prefer.

2 WITH THE SAME BRUSH, paint the leaves next, working the central outline and the smaller side leaves and then filling in. Apply two coats and leave to dry.

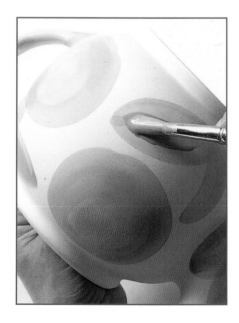

4 WITH A FINE BRUSH, paint a black circle in the center of the roses and then a black swirl within that, working quickly and trying to keep your lines as flowing and fluid as possible. (Rehearsing the line beforehand while holding the brush over the bisque will help the final brush stroke.) Paint the central spine of each leaf and then outline it with loop-shaped strokes. The petals of the roses are painted as semicircles around the center. One coat only is needed of this.

3 WITH A MEDIUM ROUND brush, apply two coats of the turquoise between the flowers and leaves. A small area can be left unpainted around flowers and leaves to add interest and movement.

Oak and Acorn Bowl

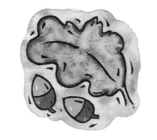

Ornella Galuccio

Fall is captured in this elegant bowl. A riot of oak leaves covers the outside and inside, and a scattering of acorns completes the pattern.

Delicate sponging in golden yellow adds texture to the design. The extra detail on the acorns is added with a sgraffito tool. This is an ideal pattern to work freehand, because the leaf shapes can be drawn quite freely and the acorns popped into the spaces. Drawing the leaves over and around the rim helps to unify the inside and outside. You could work a different design for each of the seasons.

YOU WILL NEED

BISQUEWARE PLATE

UNDERGLAZE PAINTS IN COLORS LISTED BELOW

PENCIL

FINE ROUND BRUSH

MEDIUM ROUND BRUSH

SGRAFFITO TOOL

NATURAL SPONGE

COLOR KEY

BEIGE

MEDIUM BROWN

DARK BROWN

BRIGHT GREEN

GOLDEN YELLOW

1 DRAW THE LEAVES freehand all over the bowl, some curving over the rim, and all around the same size. You can trace the shape from the Templates section if you wish. Draw the acorns in singles or pairs in the spaces, leaving the central well clear. Paint three coats of beige underglaze on the acorns, using a fine brush. Allow the color to dry thoroughly between coats.

2 USING THE SAME brush, paint three coats of medium brown on all the acorn cups. Take a sharp wooden or metal sgraffito tool, and scratch the crosshatching on the acorns—try this out on a piece of waste bisque first—so that you can see the body color of the bowl through the underglaze. Use dark brown underglaze to outline the acorns and cups.

3 PAINT THE OAK leaves in bright green with a medium-size brush, working three coats of color. Next, work some of the texture onto the leaves, using medium brown. Outline about half of each leaf, and paint some speckles by dabbing the brush around the outside edge.

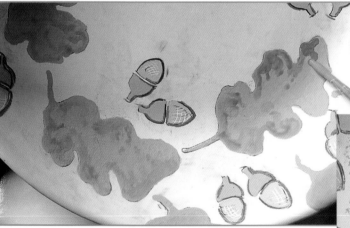

4 USING THE SAME brush, outline the oak leaves in dark brown, varying the pressure on the brush to give the leaves a realistic finish. For extra effect, paint a couple of stem details on each leaf.

5 DIP A SMALL, natural sponge in golden yellow underglaze and press it lightly onto the undecorated areas, changing the direction of the sponge as you work. Leave a little white space around the motifs, and work a deeper coat of color in the center of the bowl.

Child's Sheep *Plate*

Sharon Clark

What child wouldn't be overjoyed to be given this plate decorated with the most irresistible sheep ever? With a mixture of stripes, swirls and polkadots, it's great fun to paint as well. A name or personal message could be added to make it an ideal wall plate or incentive to help a child finish meals. The colors could be reworked to accommodate someone's favorites, or an even wilder palette could be used if pastels are not to your taste. However you do it, it is sure to raise a smile.

YOU WILL NEED

BISQUEWARE PLATE

UNDERGLAZE PAINTS IN COLORS LISTED BELOW

ACETATE

FELT-TIP PEN FOR MARKING ON ACETATE

CRAFT KNIFE OR SCISSORS

PENCIL

SMALL SPONGE

FINE BRUSH

COLOR KEY

LAVENDER

PINK

CHARTREUSE

TURQUOISE

BLACK

1. USING THE TEMPLATES IN the Templates section, trace the border, head, body, and legs onto pieces of acetate with a felt-tip pen. Cut out the shapes with a craft knife or scissors; the pieces of acetate with the shapes removed will be used as stencils. With a pencil also draw the shapes on the plate, as a guide, making sure the body is fairly central.

2. POSITION THE ACETATE OVER the drawn image, load a small sponge with lavender paint and use it to stencil the body. Be careful that the paint doesn't seep under the stencil. When dry, position the stencil for the head. Load the sponge with pink and stencil the head. Stencil the legs next using chartreuse. Finally, stencil the chartreuse border. One good, even coat of each sponged color is all that is needed, as it is thicker than paint applied with a brush.

3. WITH A FINE BRUSH, paint the grass in turquoise, making small brush strokes from the sheep's mouth outward and from the base of the legs upward. Two coats may be needed if the color is very pale.

4. USING THE FINE BRUSH, add black outlines for the sheep's head, mouth, eyes, and body. Paint the stripes on the legs and the curls in the coat, penciling them in first if you prefer. Begin at the outside edge of the body and do black swirls of varying sizes all over the area. The occasional swirl that is too small or the wrong way around will not matter.

This cheery mug is just the thing to relieve that Monday-morning feeling. Morning coffee will never be dull with these warm colors and textures. Heart motifs have long been a popular decorative symbol but they seem to be enjoying a revival on everything from furnishings to wrought-iron furniture, as they are adaptable to almost any material or medium. We have used hearts here in a stencil technique to create depth and a textural quality which is difficult to achieve with a paintbrush. A set of mugs could be worked in different colorways, such as yellow with green, orange with red, and red with blue, keeping the motifs the same and changing only the colors.

Heart Mug

Jo Wood

YOU WILL NEED

BISQUEWARE MUG

UNDERGLAZE PAINTS IN COLORS LISTED BELOW

LARGE FAN BRUSH

TILE

COARSE NATURAL SPONGE

ACETATE

FELT-TIP PEN FOR MARKING ON ACETATE

CRAFT KNIFE OR SCISSORS

SYNTHETIC SPONGE

COLOR KEY

BRIGHT YELLOW

GOLDEN YELLOW

ORANGE

LIGHT ORANGE

LIGHT RED

1 USE A LARGE FAN brush to paint the inside of the mug well with two coats of bright yellow. Pour some bright yellow and some golden yellow onto a tile. Working with a coarse natural sponge, apply one good coat of bright yellow.

2 WHEN THIS IS DRY, use the same sponge to apply a coat of golden yellow, only half covering the bright yellow. To get a really interesting texture, twist the sponge when lifting it off and change its position each time you reapply the paint. If you sponge too heavily in this color, a light coat of bright yellow can be applied to even the tones.

3 USING THE TEMPLATE IN the Templates section and a felt-tip pen, trace a heart shape onto acetate; cut it out with a craft knife or scissors. Make sure the shape will not be too high or too wide to complete the pattern. Hold the acetate stencil in place on the mug, starting near the handle, and apply a coat of orange using the natural sponge. Lift the acetate off carefully, making sure you do not smudge the wet color. When dry, repeat three more hearts evenly spaced around the mug. When they are all dry, sponge them again with a light coat of light orange.

4 CUT A SMALLER HEART stencil from acetate to decorate the inside of the mug. Sponge one coat in orange and a second in light orange to keep the same effect as the outside.

5 CUT A CIRCLE, ½in (1cm), from the synthetic sponge. Use it to sponge a single coat of light red between the hearts at the base. Also sponge a row of light red circles down the handle, keeping the spacing regular.

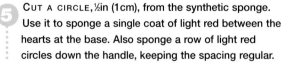

Practical and smart, this butter dish brings a bit of the country to your breakfast table. A pair of Fresian cows adorns the top of

Butter Dish
with Cows

Sharon Clark

the lid, while a border pattern of flowers and grasses runs around the sides. This is a good project for those with an eye for detail, but the use of an underglaze pencil means that not all the outlines have to be painted. The pencil gives even more of a hand-made feel to the work and is also useful where a solid black line would be too severe. This could be the start of a breakfast service—a large milk pitcher, for example, could be decorated with a whole herd of cattle.

YOU WILL NEED

BISQUEWARE BUTTER DISH

UNDERGLAZE PAINTS IN COLORS LISTED BELOW

PENCIL

TRACING PAPER

CARBON PAPER (OPTIONAL)

MEDIUM ROUND BRUSH

SMALL ROUND BRUSH

FINE BRUSH

SHARP BLACK UNDERGLAZE PENCIL

COLOR KEY

BLACK

PINK

LIGHT GREEN

DARK GREEN

YELLOW

RED

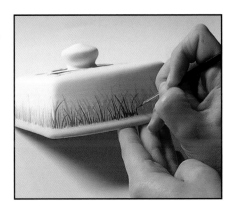

2 USING A SMALL round brush, paint the nose and udder of each cow pink. Again, three coats of color will be needed.

1 TRACE THE TEMPLATE from the Templates section and transfer the cow outlines using the tracing method or carbon paper (see Basic Techniques). Be careful to set the image down straight on the lid. With a medium brush, paint the black areas on the cows; three coats will be needed to get solid coverage.

3 NOW USE A fine brush to paint blades of grass around the sides of the lid in light green, working from the base upward. Add some dark green strokes with the same brush.

5 FINALLY, TAKE A sharp underglaze pencil and draw the outline and details of each cow. They change very little in the firing and retain the penciled effect. Be careful not to smudge the lines at this stage. With a medium brush, paint the rims of the lid and base with two coats of light green.

4 NOW ADD LITTLE yellow and red flowers at the top of the grass with the small round brush. Also paint a small area of grass and flowers around each cow's feet, using the same colors as on the sides of the lid.

Wax Resist Square Platter

Jo Wood

With its contemporary shape and equally modern decoration, this platter would look stunning on a table—or a wall—in any modern home. It is also great for anyone who likes a piece of work to progress quickly. The wax resist method gives a clean contrast between the warm colors of the squares and the cooler body color. The colors could be altered to match any decor, and the pattern could easily be adapted to suit a vase, bowl, plate, or mug.

YOU WILL NEED

SQUARE BISQUEWARE PLATTER

UNDERGLAZE PAINTS IN COLORS LISTED BELOW

PENCIL

RULER

MEDIUM FLAT BRUSH

DETERGENT

FACIAL TISSUE

WAX RESIST LIQUID

LARGE FAN BRUSH

SPONGE STICK

COLOR KEY

ORANGE

LIGHT RED

DARK RED

MEDIUM BLUE

2 THE SAME BRUSH IS used to apply the wax resist liquid. To prevent it from getting clogged up with wax, dip the brush in detergent and wipe off the excess with a facial tissue. When the colored squares are completely dry, paint one even coat of wax on each. Try not to go beyond the edges or there will be white lines around the colors.

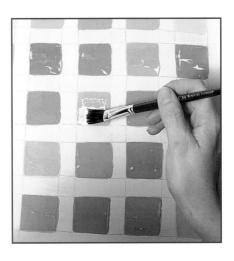

1 ON THE BASE OF the platter, mark out a grid in pencil, five squares by five squares, leaving gaps about half a square wide between them. With a medium flat brush and orange paint, fill in the squares in the center diagonal row and the single squares at the other two corners. Paint each square with three coats for a good depth of color. Now use light red to paint the diagonal rows on either side of the central one, and the diagonal rows inside the single orange squares. Use dark red for the remaining diagonal rows. All of these colors will need three coats.

3 USING A LARGE FAN BRUSH, paint the entire outside of the platter blue. Make sure that the wax is dry and then apply blue between all the painted squares, using the same brush. Over the waxed areas the paint will simply sit on the surface rather than soaking in.

4 LOAD THE FAN BRUSH WELL with blue and paint the inside rim using broad strokes. Give all the blue areas two more coats of paint to achieve a good depth of color. The background color left on the waxed areas will burn away in the firing along with the wax.

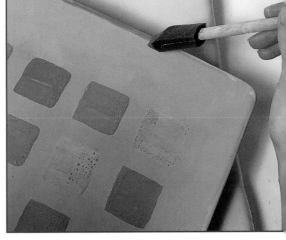

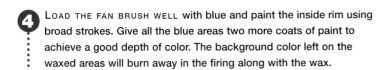

5 A SPONGE STICK IS USED to finish the edges of the platter, as it holds a larger amount of color than a traditional brush and leaves no brush marks. Dip it into the blue and, using it in the same way as a brush, paint the edges.

Arabesque Cup & Saucer

Steven Jenkins

Perfect for cappuccino, a large cup and saucer decorated with this lively pattern based on leaves and seeds make striking additions to a collection of nineteenth-century blue and white china, yet are equally at home in a modern setting. Just one color—royal blue—is used, creating an interesting effect where the brush strokes cross. The pattern builds up quickly and easily and can be adapted to almost any shape. The freedom of the pattern allows you to fill in any spaces with a lively sprig or a dot or two. If desired, the inside of the cup and the well of the saucer could also be decorated.

YOU WILL NEED

LARGE BISQUEWARE
CUP AND SAUCER

UNDERGLAZE PAINT IN COLOR
LISTED BELOW

PENCIL

LARGE ROUND BRUSH WITH A GOOD
POINT

SMALL ROUND BRUSH

COLOR KEY

ROYAL BLUE

2 USING A LARGE BRUSH with a good point, paint the swirls on the cup and saucer in a confident, fluid motion. Start each swirl with light pressure to give a fine line, then gradually apply more pressure for the thicker part. As you lift the brush off at the end of each stroke, ease the pressure to give the rough edge which is characteristic of hand-painted work. Pencil in half-moon shapes on the handle, then paint them in.

1 DIVIDE THE SAUCER INTO thirds by drawing three equally spaced pencil lines from the outer rim to the well. Starting from the well, draw two bold swirls in each section with the pencil. Divide the cup into quarters with pencil lines on the outside, first from the top of the handle to the base, then on the opposite side, and finally on the left and right. Draw a large swirl in each of the quarters, making sure that they do not all face the same way.

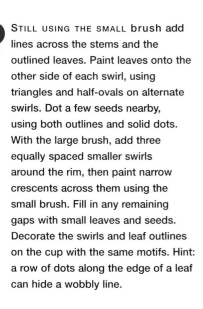

3 ON BOTH THE CUP and the saucer, use the small brush to paint the outline of a leaf next to every alternate swirl, so that the curve echoes that of the swirl. Paint curving stems next to the remaining three swirls on the saucer.

4 STILL USING THE SMALL brush add lines across the stems and the outlined leaves. Paint leaves onto the other side of each swirl, using triangles and half-ovals on alternate swirls. Dot a few seeds nearby, using both outlines and solid dots. With the large brush, add three equally spaced smaller swirls around the rim, then paint narrow crescents across them using the small brush. Fill in any remaining gaps with small leaves and seeds. Decorate the swirls and leaf outlines on the cup with the same motifs. Hint: a row of dots along the edge of a leaf can hide a wobbly line.

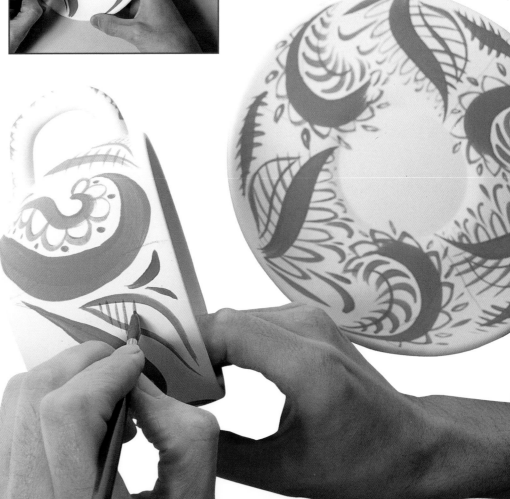

Cherry Blossom *Vase*

Steven Jenkins

With its soft coloring and design based on simple brush strokes, this elegant vase was inspired by the Orient but will suit any surroundings. The tall, angular form is perfect for the sweeping branches and cherry blossom flowers. A scattering of orange spots suggests the pollen becoming airborne. Once you have mastered the few brush strokes needed for this pattern, you will find it easy to place an Oriental-style bough and blossoms on almost anything for a simple, effective result.

YOU WILL NEED

STRAIGHT-SIDED BISQUEWARE VASE

UNDERGLAZE PAINTS IN COLORS LISTED BELOW

LARGE FAN BRUSH

LARGE ROUND BRUSH WITH A GOOD POINT

SMALL ROUND BRUSH

COLOR KEY

MINT GREEN

LIGHT TAN

AVOCADO

WHITE

MEDIUM BROWN

ORANGE

1 WITH A LARGE FAN brush, paint the neck of the vase in mint green. With the same brush and color, paint the flat sides of the vase using long downward strokes. When dry, apply a second coat.

2 NOW PAINT THE BRANCHES in light tan, using a large round brush with a good point. Work from the main stem outward, trying to make the lines flow from one another, in the same way that the plant would grow. For this step, and the following ones, use just one coat of color to keep the effect very delicate.

3 WITH THE SAME BRUSH, paint the buds and flowers white, using the brush to create each petal separately. Once again, work from the center outward, or, in the case of the buds, from the branch outward.

4 CREATE LEAVES USING TWO strokes of a small brush and avocado paint. Add a dash of the avocado between the buds and branches, too.

6 ADD THE ORANGE CENTERS of the blossoms with the same brush, making small, delicate circles. This will help the flowers look three-dimensional. As a finishing touch add "pollen" as a scattering of orange spots against the background.

5 USE THE SMALL BRUSH to paint an extra line along the center of each branch in medium brown, which will add depth and definition.

Blue Floral Pitcher

*Silva Lee
de Majo Burrows*

This blue pitcher looks at home in both traditional and modern settings. Bright open flowers are scattered all over, and there is a touch of humor in the fat bee flying between them. The design is built up from simple brush strokes; it can be worked quite quickly and easily, and adapted to suit a range of shapes. Once you have perfected the flowers, you can add them to designs of your own. The washed background could be altered to complement or match existing ceramics or a room setting.

YOU WILL NEED

BISQUEWARE JUG
UNDERGLAZE PAINTS IN COLORS LISTED BELOW
PENCIL
LARGE FAN BRUSH
LARGE ROUND BRUSH
FINE ROUND BRUSH

COLOR KEY

LIGHT BLUE

YELLOW

WHITE

ORANGE

DARK BLUE

GREEN

BLACK

1 POUR SOME LIGHT blue underglaze onto a tile and dilute slightly, to increase the flow. Use a large, fan-shape brush to paint one good coat of color over the outside and the inside rim. Try to work in bold, even strokes, and keep the underglaze a similar consistency throughout. Leave to dry thoroughly. Mark out circles on the body of the jug with a pencil, using the photograph as reference for spacing. Draw the bee under the lip of the jug.

2 USING A LARGE brush with a good point, paint the center of each flower with a good layer of bright yellow. You may need two or three coats to cover the blue. With the same brush, begin to paint the petals—work in from the outer edge, pressing fully at the outside, and lifting your brush as you near the center. Paint these strokes only once, because adding another layer will give a messy effect. Work the flowers randomly in white, orange, and dark blue.

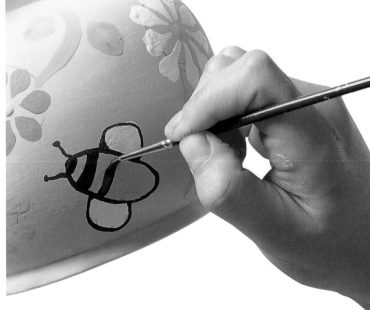

3 WORK THE STEMS and leaves in green underglaze, again using the large brush. These can be worked as "fillers" to cover a large area of background color, but still need to be fairly evenly placed around the jug. Start with the tip of the leaf and little pressure on the bisque, increase the pressure near the base, and lift the brush as you near the flower. Repeat to complete the other half of the leaf. Paint the stems in the larger free areas with a single, flowing stroke.

4 PAINT THE BEE'S body in three coats of orange underglaze. Work the wings in two or three coats of white, and when dry, outline the body and wings in black, using a fine brush. Paint the antennae, and then work the stripes with small vertical dashes to create the impression of a "furry" texture.

Luster Fish-Motif Box & Lid

Steven Jenkins

This attractive box employs platinum luster to capture the shimmering iridescence of the undersea world. Against a background of blue and green, the fish are built up in the platinum luster over a blue outline, using swift brush strokes that create a feeling of movement. Incorporating a shoal of smaller fish swimming around the box, the design makes full use of the shape of the piece, but it could be adapted to fit a range of items for a bathroom with a marine theme. An alternative to the luster would be a strong white applied over the background color.

YOU WILL NEED

BISQUEWARE BOX WITH LID

UNDERGLAZE PAINTS IN
COLORS LISTED BELOW

PLATINUM LUSTER

LARGE FAN BRUSH

PENCIL

SMALL ROUND BRUSH

MEDIUM ROUND BRUSH

MINERAL SPIRITS

FACIAL TISSUES

COLOR KEY

MEDIUM BLUE

SEA GREEN

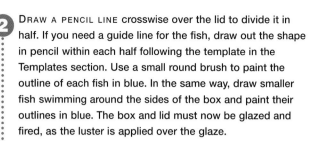

2 DRAW A PENCIL LINE crosswise over the lid to divide it in half. If you need a guide line for the fish, draw out the shape in pencil within each half following the template in the Templates section. Use a small round brush to paint the outline of each fish in blue. In the same way, draw smaller fish swimming around the sides of the box and paint their outlines in blue. The box and lid must now be glazed and fired, as the luster is applied over the glaze.

1 WORKING WITH A LARGE fan brush well loaded with color, paint a coat of medium blue all over the outside of both the box and the lid. When the first coat is dry, paint an equal amount of green over the blue. Leave to dry.

3 CLEAN THE SMALL ROUND brush and also a medium round brush in mineral spirits. Wipe facial tissues soaked in mineral spirits over the box and lid, to remove any grease or dirt that would resist the luster.

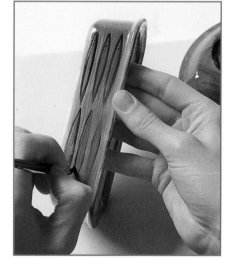

4 WHEN COMPLETELY DRY, USE the medium brush and the luster to paint the body of each fish on the lid in two strokes, following the blue guide line. The mouth and tail are painted with small curved strokes.

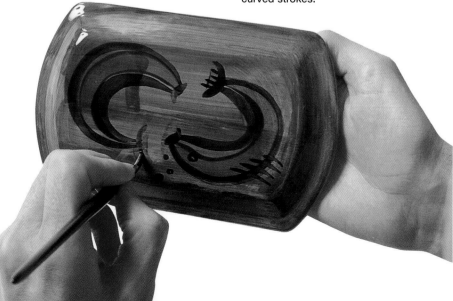

5 USING THE SMALL BRUSH, paint freehand fish on the sides of the box with two swift strokes and a dot for the eye. Any details required for the fish on the lid, such as the bubbles, are also done with this brush. The box and lid will now need a second firing, to make the luster permanent.

Leopard-Skin Plate

Sue Taylor

Leopard spots are always popular, running the gamut from kitsch to high-fashion designer branding. Our plate uses simple techniques to emulate nature's camouflage—but this is one piece that you will not want to hide! An ideal centerpiece for a living room table, this plate will provoke comment from all your visitors. The design is so adaptable that it will work on almost any surface—imagine a coffee set, for example. The color could also be adjusted to fit with your décor: yellow with gold or slate gray with charcoal also look stunning.

YOU WILL NEED

BISQUEWARE PLATE

UNDERGLAZE PAINTS IN COLORS LISTED BELOW

LATEX

PENCIL (OPTIONAL)

LARGE FAN BRUSH

FETTLING TOOL OR BLUNT CRAFT KNIFE

FINE BRUSH

TILE (OPTIONAL)

COLOR KEY

TAN

MEDIUM BROWN

BLACK

2 WHEN THE LATEX IS dry, use a large fan brush to apply a tan undercoat. Lifting the brush at the edge of the color will give the characterful "shaggy" effect. Leave small areas undecorated as in the photograph. Only one coat of color is necessary.

1 THE WHITE SPOTS ARE created by painting latex over the plate. You may find it easier to draw some of the design first. The light areas have fewer spots than the darker, bolder areas. Wash your brush in hot soapy water immediately after applying the latex, to protect the bristles.

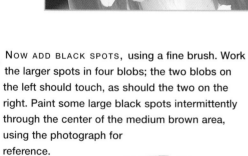

3 APPLY MEDIUM BROWN IN the same way, leaving a good deal of the tan areas showing. Do not paint on the white areas. When the paint has dried, use a fettling tool or blunt craft knife to peel off the latex, revealing the clean bisque underneath. Make sure you remove all the latex at this stage.

4 NOW ADD BLACK SPOTS, using a fine brush. Work the larger spots in four blobs; the two blobs on the left should touch, as should the two on the right. Paint some large black spots intermittently through the center of the medium brown area, using the photograph for reference.

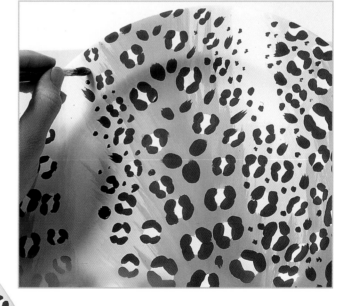

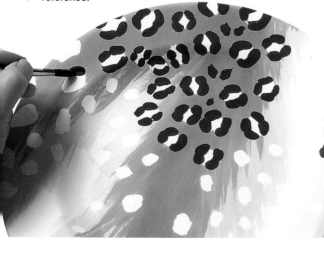

5 FINALLY, ADD THE SMALLER spots nearer the white areas, using the fine brush. Small black dots are the only pattern needed in the white areas and should fade to nothing. Practice these strokes on a tile if you wish.

Rooster Pitcher

Sharon Clark

This charming pitcher, with a colorful rooster standing out against a delicate speckled background, is sure to provoke comments and compliments. The shape of the rooster follows that of the pitcher, and neat areas of color worked in elegant brush strokes are outlined in a simple fine, black line. The project requires some patience but is worth the effort. It is also a good way of using latex resist and of producing a speckled background.

YOU WILL NEED

BISQUEWARE PITCHER

UNDERGLAZE PAINTS IN COLORS LISTED BELOW

PENCIL

TRACING PAPER

LARGE ROUND BRUSH

LATEX RESIST

DETERGENT

TILE

OLD TOOTHBRUSH

FETTLING TOOL OR OTHER SHARP OBJECT SUCH AS A PENCIL

MEDIUM ROUND BRUSH

FINE ROUND BRUSH

COLOR KEY

BLUE

LIGHT BLUE

GOLDEN YELLOW

RED

TEAL BLUE

BLACK

2 WHEN THE LATEX is completely dry, pour a little blue paint onto a tile. Dip a toothbrush in it and flick paint onto the pitcher by running your finger over the bristles. Continue to flick the blue on until you have covered the body of the pitcher fairly evenly, and then add a few spatters of teal blue for extra texture.

1 TRACE THE ROOSTER from the Templates section and transfer its outline to the pitcher (see Basic Techniques), making sure the position is correct. Using a large brush, paint an even coat of latex resist within the rooster outline. Also mask off a couple of feather shapes near the rooster's feet. Wash your brush in detergent and hot water as soon as you finish.

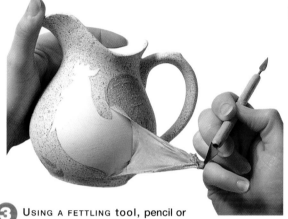

3 USING A FETTLING tool, pencil or other sharp object, dig into the latex until it starts to pull away from the bisque. When there is enough to hold between your fingers, pull gently until all the latex is free. Check the edges to make sure there is no latex left.

4 WITH A MEDIUM brush, start painting the solid areas of the rooster, painting each area in the direction in which the feathers would grow. Use light blue for the neck, golden yellow for the breast, beak, and feet, and red for the wattle and comb, applying three coats to each area. The comb and wattle may need to be painted with a small brush to achieve the fine detail.

6 WITH A FINE brush, add the black outlines around the head and feet, and also add little lines across the feet to give a ridged effect. Outline the neck, wing and tail feathers in black: start at the furthest tip and work upward, lifting your brush slowly off the pitcher. Finish off the rim with small strokes in blue and teal blue, using a medium brush.

5 WITH THE MEDIUM BRUSH, paint the teal blue tail feathers, using the photograph as a guide. Use the same brush and color to shade the ends of the neck feathers. Shade the wing feathers with a single coat red, again with the medium brush, and also paint a coat of red over the feet. Add the little feathers at the rooster's feet, in various colors, using a fine brush.

With its deep blue background and heavenly border of dots and snowflakes, this plate instantly evokes a winter sky. An easy-to-paint design, it utilizes

Snowflakes
Plate

Sarina de Majo &
Silva Lee de Majo Burrows

the wax resist technique and can be worked in a flash. A dinner set would create a stunning table display, as would a dessert set for serving ice cream or sherbet. Painting the design in a mixture of blues, greens, and grays could enhance the pattern and give it endless decorative scope. Sponging could also be added for depth.

YOU WILL NEED

BISQUEWARE LAMPBASE
UNDERGLAZE PAINTS IN COLORS
LISTED BELOW
PENCIL
LARGE FAN BRUSH
SMALL ROUND BRUSH

COLOR KEY

DARK BLUE

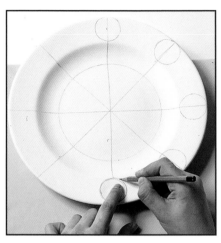

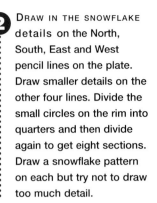

2 DRAW IN THE SNOWFLAKE details on the North, South, East and West pencil lines on the plate. Draw smaller details on the other four lines. Divide the small circles on the rim into quarters and then divide again to get eight sections. Draw a snowflake pattern on each but try not to draw too much detail.

1 USING A PENCIL AND ruler, divide the plate into quarters. Divide these sections once more so you have eight sections. (Snowflakes really have six sides but eight work better for design purposes, as they fill the space better.) Cut out a small circle in acetate or cardboard, just slightly smaller than the width of the plate's rim. Use this to draw round, marking a circle on the plate's rim at the end of each pencil line.

3 DIP A SMALL ROUND brush in detergent and wipe off the excess on a facial tissue. Use it to paint one good, even coat of wax along all the pencil lines. Add some spots or blobs of wax in the spaces between the snowflakes as shown. The wax sometimes leaves lumps on the painted area, but do not try to remove these as they will then not resist when painted.

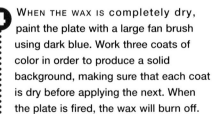

4 WHEN THE WAX IS completely dry, paint the plate with a large fan brush using dark blue. Work three coats of color in order to produce a solid background, making sure that each coat is dry before applying the next. When the plate is fired, the wax will burn off.

Wax Resist Flowers

Bowl

Jo Wood

The technique of wax resist is employed again here, this time giving a sharp contrast between the jewel-bright flowers and the glossy black of the background. Two shades of green give depth to the foliage, and a clever mix of colors gives all the flowers a three-dimensional look. The pattern could be simplified for a vase or used with a different-colored background to coordinate with a particular theme.

YOU WILL NEED

BISQUEWARE BOWL

UNDERGLAZE PAINTS IN COLORS LISTED BELOW

PENCIL

MEDIUM ROUND BRUSH

DETERGENT

FACIAL TISSUE

WAX RESIST LIQUID

LARGE FAN BRUSH

COLOR KEY

LILAC

LAVENDER

VIOLET

YELLOW-ORANGE

ORANGE

LIGHT RED

DARK RED

CHARTREUSE

LEAF GREEN

DARK GREEN

BLACK

1 USING A PENCIL, SKETCH bunches of flower heads around the outside of the bowl, spacing them equally. Now pencil in the bunches of flowers on the inside, making sure they "flow" with the pattern on the outside. Try to keep all the flowers roughly the same size.

2 THE FLOWERS ARE PAINTED from the centers outward, using a medium round brush. For some bunches use the lilac, lavender, and violet; for others use two coats of yellow-orange and one of orange; and for a third type use two coats of light red and one of dark red. Paint each flower with the first color, then go over it with the second shade (or another layer of the first), followed by the third shade. With each layer, leave some of the previous coat uncovered.

3 USE THE SAME BRUSH to apply the wax resist. First dip the brush in detergent and wipe off the excess with a facial tissue. Paint one even coat of wax over each flower using the same brush strokes as for the colors. Do not try to cover the whole petal with the wax as the design could look labored.

4 WHEN THE WAX IS dry, use a large fan brush to paint areas of chartreuse and leaf green beneath the flowers and in bands between each cluster. Start your strokes at the bottom of the bowl and work upward. Once again, avoid covering all of the underneath color when applying the second one. Introduce some variety by giving some areas two coats of chartreuse and one of leaf green, and vice versa. Using the same brush, apply a coat of dark green to cover about half of the lighter green area.

5 DIP A MEDIUM ROUND brush in detergent, wipe off the excess with a facial tissue, and then paint wax lines from the base through the flowers to form stalks. The more wax you apply, the more greenery there will be in the finished piece.

6 WHEN THE WAX IS dry, paint the outside of the bowl black using the large fan brush. Repeat this until you have three solid coats of color, then paint the inside of the bowl in the same way. To finish off the rim neatly, use a sponge stick and apply three coats of black.

Dolphin Vase

The elegant curves of this vase demand an equally graceful design, and what better image than a family of dolphins, leaping out of the sea in perfect

Sue Taylor

unison? As a project this vase offers a challenge or two, because a number of different techniques are employed to achieve the final result. As well as having learned new ways of decorating pottery, you will have a wonderful piece of work—which will make an ideal gift if you can bear to part with it.

YOU WILL NEED

BISQUEWARE VASE

UNDERGLAZE PAINTS IN COLORS
LISTED BELOW

PENCIL

TRACING PAPER

TAPE

SMALL ROUND BRUSH

DETERGENT

FACIAL TISSUE

LATEX RESIST

TILE

LARGE FAN BRUSH

SMALL PIECE OF SPONGE

STYLUS

LARGE SGRAFFITO TOOL

COLOR KEY

LIGHT GREEN

LIGHT BLUE

LIGHT GRAY

MEDIUM BLUE

1 TRACE THE DOLPHINS from the Templates section and tape the tracing to the center-front of the vase. Transfer the design to the bisque and remove the tracing.

2 DIP A SMALL ROUND brush in detergent and wipe off the excess on a facial tissue. Use the brush to apply one coat of latex resist over the dolphins, covering them entirely.

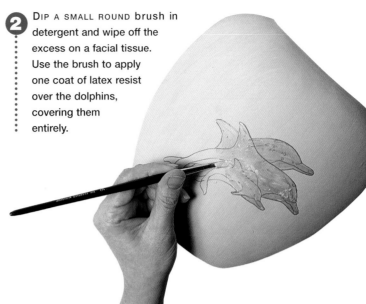

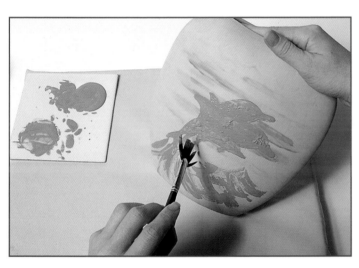

3 WHEN THE LATEX IS completely dry, pour a little light green and light blue paint onto a tile. Using a large fan brush, paint horizontal brush strokes in both colors, to give a random effect. Go over the whole vase, making sure the central area is well covered and fading the color away toward the edges.

4 WHEN THE BACKGROUND COLORS are dry, you can peel away the latex. Dig into the latex gently with a sharp point such as the end of a pencil—the film should pull away from the vase quite easily. Pull it off using your finger and thumb, and brush away any loose or flaky paint.

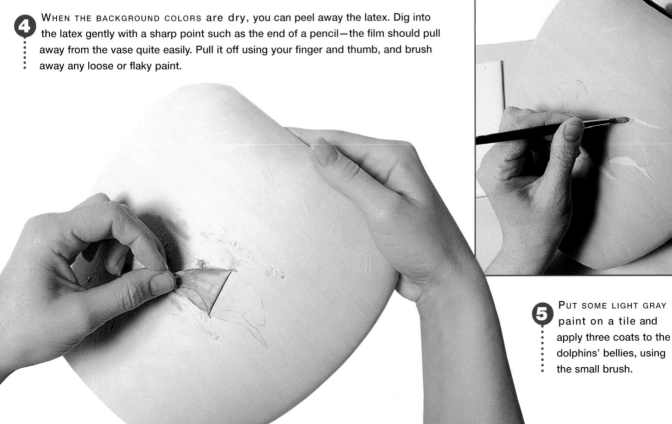

5 PUT SOME LIGHT GRAY paint on a tile and apply three coats to the dolphins' bellies, using the small brush.

6 REPEAT WITH MEDIUM BLUE for the dolphins' backs. Don't worry if the edges are not perfectly neat at this stage.

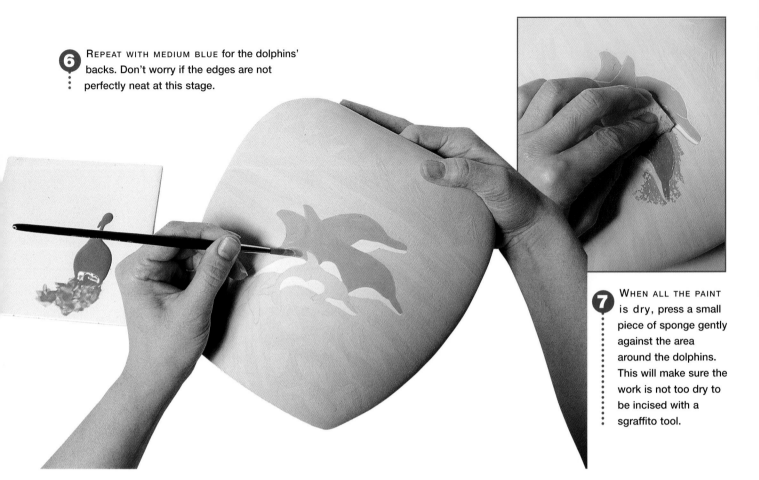

7 WHEN ALL THE PAINT is dry, press a small piece of sponge gently against the area around the dolphins. This will make sure the work is not too dry to be incised with a sgraffito tool.

8 USING A STYLUS, LIGHTLY draw the outline and detail on the dolphins, including the eyes. This will help to "pull out" the figures from the background.

9 NOW USE A LARGE sgraffito tool to create the bold white highlights of the waves.

Aboriginal Round Platter

Aboriginal designs are favorites of textile designers, painters, and many craftspeople. This Aboriginal-inspired platter is ideal for the wall or a centerpiece on a table. The background texture gives extra depth and interest, and the stylized snake, with its warm, earthy palette, is far more likely to charm than to frighten. Other Aboriginal images would also be suitable, or you could try adapting Aztec or African motifs.

Sarina de Majo & Silva Lee de Majo Burrows

YOU WILL NEED

ROUND BISQUEWARE PLATTER

UNDERGLAZE PAINTS IN COLORS LISTED BELOW

PENCIL

TRACING PAPER

TAPE

SMALL FLAT BRUSH

MEDIUM ROUND BRUSH

TILE

FETTLING TOOL OR STYLUS

DETERGENT

FACIAL TISSUE

WAX RESIST

SMALL NATURAL SPONGE

OLD TOOTHBRUSH

COLOR KEY

MEDIUM BROWN

DARK BROWN

YELLOW

BEIGE

LIGHT SAND

GREEN

PURPLE

1 TRACE THE SNAKE FROM the Templates section and tape the tracing in the center of the platter. Transfer the design to the bisque and remove the tracing.

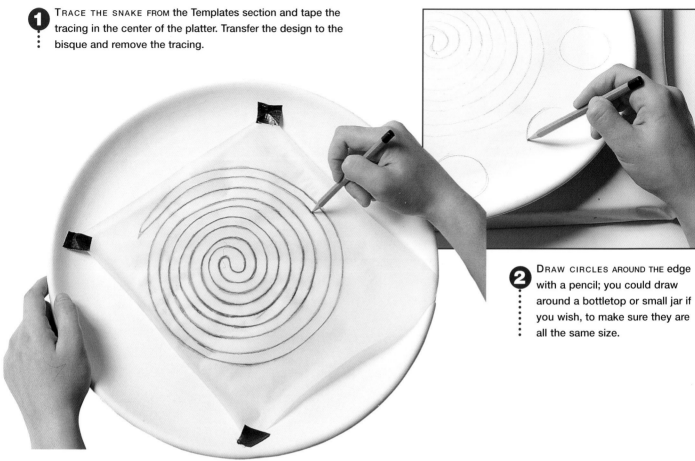

2 DRAW CIRCLES AROUND THE edge with a pencil; you could draw around a bottletop or small jar if you wish, to make sure they are all the same size.

4 PAINT THE CIRCLES AROUND the border in alternate yellow and beige, using a medium round brush. Apply three coats of each color to get solid coverage.

3 WITH A SMALL FLAT brush, paint the snake in alternate segments of mid brown and dark brown. If desired, you can draw the segments with a pencil first. Paint these three times to give a solid color.

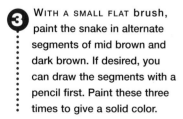

5 POUR SOME BROWN PAINT onto a tile. Dip the wrong end of a pencil into the paint, then test it on a piece of waste bisque or the edge of a tile, to make sure the paint isn't too runny. Use this to make the dots on the border circles. Make further patterns in the same way using the green and yellow paints.

7 DIP THE MEDIUM ROUND brush in detergent and wipe off the excess with a tissue. Now use it to paint a coat of wax resist onto the snake and the circles. (The wax will burn off in the firing.)

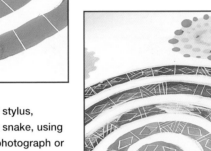

6 WITH A FETTLING TOOL or stylus, scratch the pattern on the snake, using either the patterns in the photograph or a design of your own.

8 POUR SOME LIGHT SAND paint onto a tile or shallow dish. Dip a small natural sponge in the paint and lightly sponge on an even coat of paint all over the design.

9 FOR EXTRA TEXTURE, dip a toothbrush in some purple paint and flick the paint over the surface with your finger. Try to achieve an even coverage of speckles, with no area neglected and no area overworked.

10 FINALLY, USE THE PENCIL-END method (see step 5) to add further dots around the rim and in a wavy line weaving in and out of the circles. This detailing will help to join all the elements together.

Wedding Platter

Steven Jenkins

What could be a nicer gift for a friend's wedding than a hand-painted platter? This romantic image of the couple surrounded by confetti is outlined quickly in black and then "tinted" with light brush strokes of pastel shades, to create an effect resembling watercolors. The confetti is painted in solid colors to add to the decorative effect. There is plenty of scope to personalize the piece with the bride's and groom's names and the date of the wedding.

YOU WILL NEED

BISQUEWARE PLATTER
UNDERGLAZE PAINTS IN COLORS
LISTED BELOW
PENCIL
FINE BRUSH
SMALL ROUND BRUSH
MEDIUM ROUND BRUSH

COLOR KEY

BLACK

RED

GREEN

PEACH

BLUE

LEMON

GRAY

BROWN

1 DRAW THE CENTRAL MOTIF of the couple, tracing it from the Templates section if desired. Try to position the faces as centrally as possible.

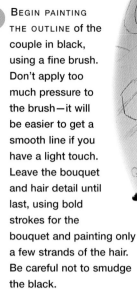

2 BEGIN PAINTING THE OUTLINE of the couple in black, using a fine brush. Don't apply too much pressure to the brush—it will be easier to get a smooth line if you have a light touch. Leave the bouquet and hair detail until last, using bold strokes for the bouquet and painting only a few strands of the hair. Be careful not to smudge the black.

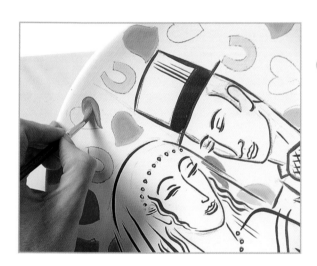

3 WITH A SMALL ROUND brush, paint the confetti shapes around the edge of the platter, adding an extra motif anywhere that there is a space. The colors are red for hearts, green for circles, peach for horseshoes and blue for the bells. Try to distribute the shapes and colors evenly. Three coats will be needed on all the confetti shapes. Also paint red roses in the bouquet and the groom's button-hole.

4 NOW PAINT THE CENTRAL motif. With a medium brush apply one coat of peach on the skin areas. Just use light strokes—there is no need to completely fill in the area. Use the same technique for applying lemon to the bride's veil and dress, and then also add some lemon to the bouquet and to the groom's cravat. Fill in the groom's hat and coat with one coat of gray, his waistcoat with blue, and hair with brown. Finally, add the greenery to the bouquet and button-hole.

Sgraffito Canister

This bright and cheery canister is just right for a modern kitchen or bathroom. Bold stripes reminiscent of ethnic textiles are decorated with repeat patterns in a method known as sgraffito. This pattern is achieved by actually carving through the painted colors to reveal the pottery color underneath. We have used spirals, wavy lines, and dots but these could just as easily be letters or more complex patterns. This is an ideal way of decorating if you have a limited palette of colors to work with.

*Sarina de Majo &
Silva Lee de Majo Burrows*

YOU WILL NEED

BISQUEWARE CANISTER

UNDERGLAZE PAINTS IN COLORS LISTED BELOW

PENCIL

WHEEL

LARGE FLAT BRUSH

STYLUS

COLOR KEY

TEAL BLUE

LIGHT BLUE

CHARTREUSE

ORANGE

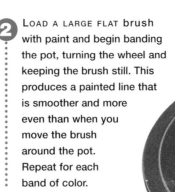

2 LOAD A LARGE FLAT brush with paint and begin banding the pot, turning the wheel and keeping the brush still. This produces a painted line that is smoother and more even than when you move the brush around the pot. Repeat for each band of color.

1 WITH A PENCIL, ROUGHLY mark out the width of the stripes down one side of the canister. It will be easier to make the bands fairly wide, as you will be working with a broad brush, and each band needs to be wide enough to include a pattern. Place the canister centrally on a wheel and, holding the pencil against the body, turn the wheel. This will give you a straight guide line around the pot. Continue until all the bands are drawn.

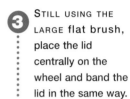

3 STILL USING THE LARGE flat brush, place the lid centrally on the wheel and band the lid in the same way.

4 SGRAFITTO IS BEST WORKED off the wheel, so hold the base comfortably in your hand for this stage. The pattern is scratched into the bisque with a stylus, which cuts through without shattering the color, leaving a clean line. Incise the patterns row by row. They can be roughed out in pencil first if required.

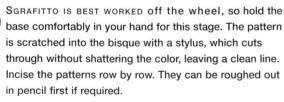

5 SCRATCH SIMILAR PATTERNS ON the lid, bearing in mind that squares will have to taper inward to fit in the banded area. The button on the lid is an ideal spot for a spiral or star.

Lusterware Espresso Cup & Saucer

Steven Jenkins

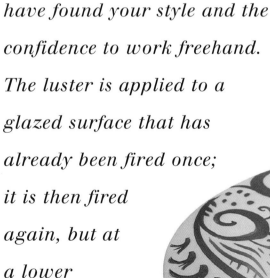

On traditional lusterware rich, iridescent effects were achieved by mixing metallic oxides such as gold, silver or copper with yellow ocher. Nineteenth century lusterware was often combined with transfer patterns in blue or black, but here the luster speaks for itself with an all-over pattern that develops from a simple framework. You may need to sketch the patterns on paper the first time, but soon you will have found your style and the confidence to work freehand. The luster is applied to a glazed surface that has already been fired once; it is then fired again, but at a lower temperature.

YOU WILL NEED

GLAZED AND FIRED BISQUEWARE
ESPRESSO CUP AND SAUCER

MEDIUM ROUND BRUSH

MINERAL SPIRITS

FELT-TIP PEN

PLATINUM LUSTER

1 CLEAN THE CUP, saucer and a medium brush with mineral spirits; leave to dry. Using a felt-tip pen, divide the saucer rim into quarters and then draw a long swirl and a short swirl in each of the sections. Draw a flower head on the front of the cup, taking the stem of the flower all the way around the cup to the base of the handle. Draw some swirling leaves from the base to "grow around" the body of the cup. The felt-tip marks will disappear during the firing process.

2 WITH THE MEDIUM brush, apply platinum luster to the swirls marked out on the saucer. Using the photograph as a guide, add small details to each of the leaves in turn until the pattern fills the rim.

4 FINALLY, ADD THE leaf detail to the cup: a stripe pattern in one, a line of dots in the next, a row of semicircles in the next, and so on. Great patterns can evolve using this method of working.

3 PAINT THE CUP in a similar manner, following the outlines of the flower first and then the stalks until you have painted in all the lines you marked out. If there is a large white area, another tendril can be added to fill the space, but do not overfill the area as some white space around a pattern is desirable.

Holly and Ivy Lampbase

Steven Jenkins

Although this project has a distinctly festive-season inspiration, the colors and styling allow it to work as a decorative object all year round. A subtle mix of blues and greens work with the body color to form a fluid design that is easy to paint and satisfying to look at. Lampbases work best with a simple design or a textured finish like sponging. A decorative base works best with a plain shade and vice-versa. With very little alteration the design could be used on a vase instead of a lampbase, or the leaf motifs could be worked into a border design for a plate or bowl.

YOU WILL NEED

BISQUEWARE LAMPBASE

UNDERGLAZE PAINTS IN COLORS LISTED BELOW

PENCIL

LARGE FAN BRUSH

SMALL ROUND BRUSH

COLOR KEY

TURQUOISE

MEDIUM GREEN

TEAL BLUE

1 DRAW FOUR PENCIL LINES from top to bottom to divide the lampbase into quarters. Now divide it vertically into eight sections using horizontal lines. Working from the base of the first line, and using the photograph as reference, draw a curved line that roughly follows a vertical line—this will become a stem. Repeat for the other three stems. The leaves on each stem will be positioned wherever horizontal lines intersect the vertical line, and the leaves will be alternately angled out to the left or right. Draw the center line of each leaf.

2 USING A LARGE FAN brush well loaded with turquoise, paint leaves coming off alternate stalks. Work from the base upward, holding the brush tight to the bisque and lifting it off slowly to give the rough texture at the end of each stroke. Two strokes will give both texture and strong color. Paint the leaves on the other stalks in medium green using the same brushwork, but only one coat.

3 WHEN THE LEAVES ARE dry, apply teal blue detailing on top. First work the larger main stems with a small brush, in sections. Pressing the brush close to the bisque halfway through the stroke gives the distinctive quality of line, increasing its width as you press harder.
Paint holly leaf outlines over the turquoise brush strokes by joining up several small crescent shapes. Add small swirls to suggest berries. One coat from a well-loaded brush will give the desired effect.

4 FOR THE IVY LEAVES, you will be painting over the medium green brush strokes. If you wish, mark the three outer points of each leaf in pencil before painting. Paint the stem, and then the outer section of the leaf. Do not worry if the outline shape is a bit larger than your green brush stroke—this will give a more loose and dynamic feel. Add a spiral tendril to balance the berries on the holly.

5 TO FINISH THE DESIGN, add a simple brush stroke to each stem at the base. This fills spaces in the design and adds continuity.

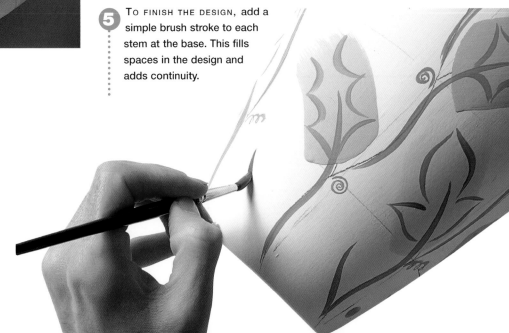

Lupin Vase

Silva Lee de Majo Burrows

This cylinder vase is decorated with such a feel for the subject matter that you can almost smell the flowers. The pattern is evocative of gardens in the 1920s and 1930s where lupins, stocks, and hollyhocks grew in borders and park displays. These were also a favorite subject on ceramics, wallpapers, and chintz fabrics of the day. We have brought the idea right up to date using a clever technique with the colors and brushes to give depth and vividness to the vase—in fact, it will look nearly as good empty as when it is filled with flowers.

YOU WILL NEED

BISQUEWARE VASE

UNDERGLAZE PAINTS IN COLORS LISTED BELOW

PENCIL (OPTIONAL)

LARGE ROUND BRUSH WITH A GOOD POINT

MEDIUM ROUND BRUSH

COLOR KEY

GREEN

PURPLE

DEEP RED

DARK BLUE

LIGHT GREEN

2 THE PURPLE FLOWERS are painted from the center of the stalk outward, using the large brush. Place the brush tip against the stem and move it a short distance, slowly increasing the pressure until the brush fibers are pushed flat against the surface. Lift the brush off. This brush stroke gives a lovely hand-painted texture and needs only one coat. Repeat this technique for all the flowers on the stalk, varying the size and length of the flowers. Twisting the brush slightly as you lift it off the surface gives an even fuller bloom.

1 WE DECIDED TO work freehand to keep the pattern as lively as possible but you may prefer to pencil in a framework of stems beforehand. Using a large brush with a good point, paint the central stem, a few leaves, and the bud at the top with green. After the tip of the brush touches the bisque, press down, varying the pressure on the bisque to produce the desired line. Use only one coat to let the texture show. Paint the other flower stems and leaves—four fitted well onto this vase.

3 PAINT THE FLOWERS on the adjacent stalk in deep red, using the large brush and the same technique. Try to make smaller buds at the top and fuller, longer flowers at the base of the flower. Work the remaining two flower stalks around the vase, either in purple and then red (with occasional buds in the other color) or mixing the red and purple on each flower stalk.

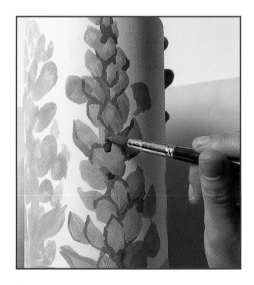

4 WITH A MEDIUM brush and using the photograph as a guide, paint one coat of dark blue shading on each flower, adding just a little shadow to the buds at the top of each stalk and larger, bolder shading as you descend. Give the buds in the center a complete outline in dark blue; buds at the edges only need a line on one side. Outline the leaves in dark blue too, and fill in any undecorated areas at the stalk's base.

5 USING THE MEDIUM brush, add light green highlights to the leaves at the base of the vase, either working along half a leaf shape or highlighting the top "spear" of the shoot. This extra layer adds texture and realism to the design.

1 THIS MODERN BOWL by Gaynor Reeve is decorated in a bold way, using colored slips, a mixture of pigments or color and wet clay that is applied onto a greenware item before it dries. You could achieve a similar effect with the bold use of underglazes: drizzle or flick color with a well-loaded brush, or use a sponge or piece of cloth to make large solid shapes of color. It is always wise to try out the technique on a small item first.

2 THIS SHALLOW BOWL by Seth Cardew uses another traditional technique: tin glaze. Here, the decoration is applied over the unfired glaze, and the colors sink through during firing. Bold use of the brush, with the minimum of drawing out beforehand, helps the freedom of the line, and a quick wash effect in a second color gives another dimension. With an extra touch of sgraffito detail on the border, this is a perfect style for a folk art or country farmhouse look.

4 THIS LARGE, HAND-THROWN fruit bowl by Daphne Carnegy uses decorated underglaze. The free placing of the apples and leaves motifs, and the naturalistic colors, work well against a strong, blue background. The white space around the images makes for a livelier feel, as do the apple segments. It is always useful to think of different ways of illustrating your chosen motif, by changing the direction, the color range, or, in the case of fruit, showing it sliced, cut in half, or peeled for variety.

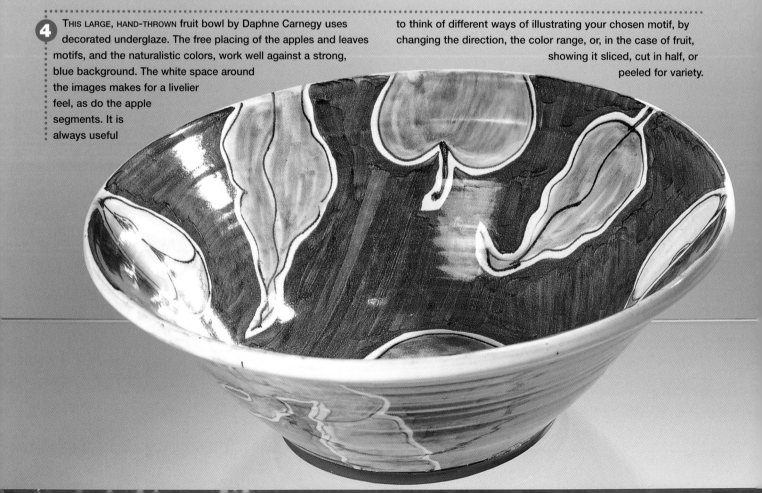

Centerpieces

3 JOHN POLLEX'S BRIGHT, contemporary-shaped platter was inspired by the work of the American abstract expressionist painters. A distinctive use of color and form works in harmony with the shape to make a modern statement, and the individual use of underglaze color, overlaying, and shading provides extra depth. To make a feature of the edge, the outside rim is decorated with a combed effect. The shape is also ideal for painting, because it has no difficult curves and edges that can make brushwork awkward, and the rim acts as a frame for the decoration in the center.

6 THIS ELEGANT VASE by Simon Thomason (bottom right) has overtones of the Red Queen in *Alice in Wonderland*. The worked underglaze in the repeat pattern of hearts in squares makes the form and decoration completely at one with each other. Patterns like this, when a repeated motif is stepped up diagonally, can fool the eye into thinking that there are far more colors than there actually are. Picking out a less obtrusive color for the rim also helps to balance the finished object. Some of the most successful patterns are very simple, but employ this kind of clever use of color.

5 PATCHWORK APPEARS TO be the inspiration for Jackie Kohler's bowl (bottom center), with alternating bands of light and dark blue underglaze worked inside, and a simple band of light blue outside. The bands inside were drawn freely for extra character, and the two colors were then "stitched" together, with small, white brush strokes worked randomly along the edges of the colors. For a finishing touch, the white brush strokes painted along the top edge bridge the gap between the outside and inside of the bowl. This is an ideal style for patterns, because you can complete it quickly without its becoming too repetitive.

Tableware

1 ON THE SIDE salad or hors d'oeuvre tray by Jackie Kohler, sponging or stippling has been used to pick out the rim in a traditional dark green. The eggplant in the well has been painted to fill the area in naturalistic colors. Scale is very important to the final result: if you are painting a radish or daisy, there is no reason to make them as small as they are in life—take as much space as you have available. Similarly, melons and pumpkins need not be life-size—a small, scatter pattern would work very well.

2 KATE BYRNE'S SUGAR bowl also employs naturalistic colors, and is painted to achieve a bold, almost watercolor finish. Loose brush strokes and a random pattern of dots in the background pull the motifs together. Yellow and red underglazes are mixed for the prickly pear, with a black outline applied in a free style for a lively feel. Leaving the inside white draws attention to the pattern. When working bowls, the pattern should not be too low down, because it may not be seen in use.

5 STYLIZED LEAF MOTIFS are the theme for this modern plate design, also by Kate Byrne. Rich gold and ocher underglaze colors are used for the background, and the leaves are worked in shades of gray. A band of green is added to the outside rim to frame the plate, helping to give the yellows more impact and also heightening the shading on the leaves. It is always a good idea to consider the dominant color on tableware. If an item will be used to eat off, bear in mind that some colors do not complement food, and could have the opposite effect: clean, natural colors are good, but some shades of blue and some darker colors do not work so well.

3 INCREDIBLE DETAIL FILLS this plate by Sue Masters: olives, asparagus, melons, and a wild mix of fruits and vegetables are scattered in an animated manner. Greenery fills the empty space, giving a harvest quality to the pattern. The colors are naturalistic, but simplified almost to a flat color, and the key line on top adds all the detail and form. Selective outlining on objects always helps to give a feeling of movement and life, and changing the thickness of the line as you paint will also help lift things off the plate.

4 WHAT BETTER BACKGROUND color for a dashing, modern butter dish than a rich yellow, with egg-yolk gold underglaze texture added with bold brush strokes. In Marlyse Michel's butter dish, the pattern of tulip heads and leaves is worked on top in red and green. The finishing touches are the handles, painted in a contemporary purple, and everything is then held together with small, swiftly painted strokes in purple on the lid. This rich palette of colors works well because there is a predominant color, and the others work around it.

6 TIN GLAZE IS used on this charming cereal bowl by Mike Levy, which has a slightly matte finish and a distinctive feel. The bowl shows good use of a restricted palette—the cat is worked in one color, a traditional, rich blue. Once the outlines are worked and dry, the color is thinned with water and used for shading. The banding complements the center design.

7 LYN O'NEILL'S SOUP bowl is painted with a pride of lions in on-glaze fired acrylic colors. These are not as durable as underglaze colors, and so are best used on decorative items. Deep yellow, orange, and light brown are used on the lions, with dark brown outlines and detail. The motifs have been designed to leave the well of the bowl and part of the rim free. The bowl has been painted in a light blue, and a finishing band of dark red has been applied to the outer rim.

Kitchenware

1 THE SQUAT JUG by Sue Masters (bottom left) is decorated with a mixture of cut fruit, olives, and flowers, to give a rich, full pattern. Leaves on the handle echo the foliage on the body. The natural underglaze palette works well against the body color of the ware. Many bisque ceramics seem white but have a cream color when glazed—this can be worked to your advantage.

2 KATE BYRNE'S JUG has stylized gooseberries and leaves against a rich, blue background. Decorated in underglazes on a traditional shape, it is a perfect item for the kitchen dresser. The fruit is painted in yellow and orange, and the leaves in green and blue-green. Fine brush work has been added in black for the gooseberry hairs and outlines, and for the serrated leaves. A wide brush was used to fill the background area, working closely but not slavishly, and the color has deepened where two or three layers have been applied. The handle is decorated in solid blue to balance the shape.

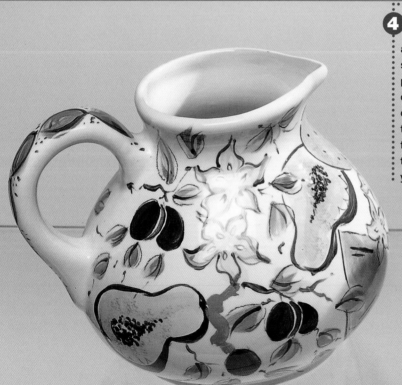

4 ON ANOTHER SQUAT jug by Sue Masters, the body color has formed the petals on the daisies. The yellow flower centers are given an extra touch of detail with red stippling using a sponge. The dark blue underglaze is then added, leaving the petals undecorated. Smaller flowers have been worked down the handle; this can be a nice area to add a flamboyant touch to your work.

3 TRADITIONAL PATTERN AND color have been used on this jug by Jackie Kohler, inspired by Italian pottery of the Renaissance. Yellow, orange, green, and blue underglaze colors have been applied in a loose style. Fine brush work in black then pulls the pattern together, and some banding on the top and bottom finishes the design. The way to retain the feel of this piece is not to overwork the outlining. This style of decoration works particularly well on larger pieces.

5 HONEY BEES FLY busily around their hive on this small soap dish by Kate Glanville. The underneath is painted in bold stripes in yellow and green underglazes, and the outer rim has a green band. The detail is kept to the base of the well of the dish, where flat colors are outlined neatly in black. There are some red flowers at the base of the design. Some practical shapes like this soap dish have ridges or other details that can be difficult to paint over, so bear them in mind when you design your decoration.

5 LYN O'NEILL'S FINE bone china jug has been decorated with an acrylic paint that is fired on-glaze. This design does not restrict your choice decorative technique. Black has been used here to great effect, centering on an updated ethnic pattern, and clever brush work has been mixed with sgraffito to form an all-over pattern. Such patterns allow you to add an extra swirl or couple of dots to fill an empty space.

Teapots & Teacups

1 A TRADITIONAL-SHAPE teapot has been brought right up to date with this great pattern by Simon Thomason. The orange background has bold red brush strokes through it; the handle is striped in purple and white, and the purple lid of the pot holds it all together. The bright colors in the vignettes, such as the cat and balloon, benefit from black underglaze surrounds, which set off the detail against the background, and sgraffito lines which link all the shapes.

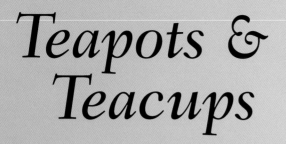

3 JANE PUMFREY'S CONTEMPORARY teapot shape is decorated with an abstract pattern of stars on a speckled background. Worked on bisque, this design uses sponging to achieve all its texture. An even coat of light green underglaze is worked all over the body and lid, and a sponge cut into a star shape is then used to apply the color details in yellow, red, blue, black, and green. For a final touch, a dark green was taken to pick out details of the shape. The lid, top rim, handle, and spout were sponged gently to give gradations of color.

4 ON-GLAZE PAINTS and gold luster give this bone china cup and saucer by Ian Morris and Kathryn Phelp a cheery, modern look. Gold and bright red can only be applied on-glaze, so this is an ideal pattern for bone china. Underglaze reds often lack real intensity, therefore it is a good idea to work them next to a color that will intensify them. The simplicity of the design here proves that you don't always have to cover every inch of space when decorating.

2 THESE TWO TIN-GLAZE cups and saucers by Mike Levy seem quite timeless. Decorated in light blue and black figurative and abstract patterns, they would sit well in almost any style of surroundings. The deep saucers echo early 19th-century teaware, and the pattern is reminiscent of the work of the Bloomsbury Group. The fine, confident line work is tinted with a little shading in light blue. A random dot pattern is used under one saucer, and banding and wavy lines on the other. Organic sprigs are worked on one cup and saucer, and simple strokes of blue are painted on both the handles.

5 ANOTHER TRADITIONAL TEAPOT shape is decorated in a contemporary manner by Kate Byrne. The bold pineapple motif is painted underglaze in a confident, free style, using yellow and red, with green for the leaves. The background, outlining, and detail are then worked in a teal blue. The lid of the teapot picks out the color of the fruit, and the handle is decorated to blend in with the body. One can be endlessly inventive with fruit motifs, so it is always worth doodling to see what you come up with.

Coffee Cups & Mugs

1 THESE TWO ESPRESSO cups by Kate Byrne (above) demonstrate how the same shape can look with different designs. The first shows a prickly pear, and you can almost see the order of the brush strokes: yellow, lime green, and dark green for the outlining and detail. The background underglaze color was then applied with a large brush, and the green lining on the edge of the saucer and the top of the cup was the last stage. The other cup and saucer have more work in them: two colors for the petals, red for the flower center, outlining, and detail, and then the background color. Once again, the lining is the last stage.

4 LYN O'NEILL'S MUG is another example of on-glaze fired acrylic color, providing the richness of the red on the poppy. Blue strokes give the shading on the petals, and black dots the center. A sprig or two of green relieves the red, and the blue of the background helps to balance this. A simple, black outline and a fine line on the rim finish off the design.

2 THE WARM PINKY-RED of the melon on Sue Masters' cappuccino cup and saucer is complemented by the cool gray of the background underglaze decoration. Painted in red, with a thin, light gray skin and a minimum of outline and detail, the melon slices have been painted as large as possible, to show off the size of the cup. Small black lines across the handle add detail and break up an undecorated area. The rim and edge of the saucer are left as body color, as are small areas of the fruit.

3 THIS MUG BY Jackie Kohler has a wonderful watercolor feel to it—the colors are hazy and soft. The mug has been divided into sections, and a basic pattern has been applied in underglaze. To keep the quality of the brush strokes, only one layer of color was used. The handle and lining at the top reflect the blue in the body.

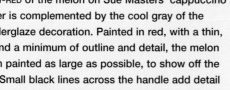

5 THE TWO LIVELY mugs by Kate Glanville (below and below left) are decorated in underglaze colors—both depend largely on the outline to hold the pattern together. Once the patterns are drawn out, the color is applied loosely in the penciled areas, and a background color is applied to the "candy" mug. The black is then applied with confident, swift brush strokes, and the whole pattern comes together.

6 SIMPLE STRIPES AND spots form the design on this conical coffee mug by Kate Glanville. Light and dark blue stripes, with occasional sgraffito detail, are broken up with rows of circles. A blue line to the rim and a brush stroke down the handle, and there you are—all done. Sometimes the simplest and quickest designs produce the best work, and experimenting with simple patterns is a great way of finding your style or strengths in pottery decoration.

TEMPLATES

The templates which follow in this section are designed to be traced or copied and enlarged. Projects which have no template here are designed to be worked freehand.

Sponged Ducks Child's Bowl, page 32.

Cat's bowl, page 36

Rosebud Vase,
page 38.

Wax Resist
Fruit Bowl with
Pears, page 40.

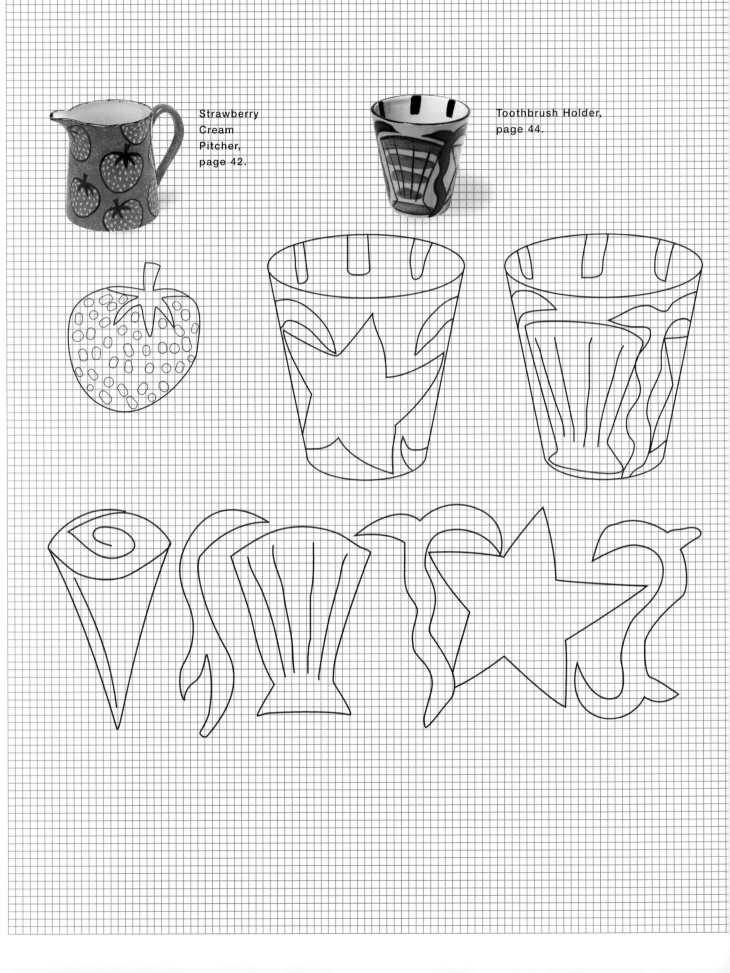

Strawberry Cream Pitcher, page 42.

Toothbrush Holder, page 44.

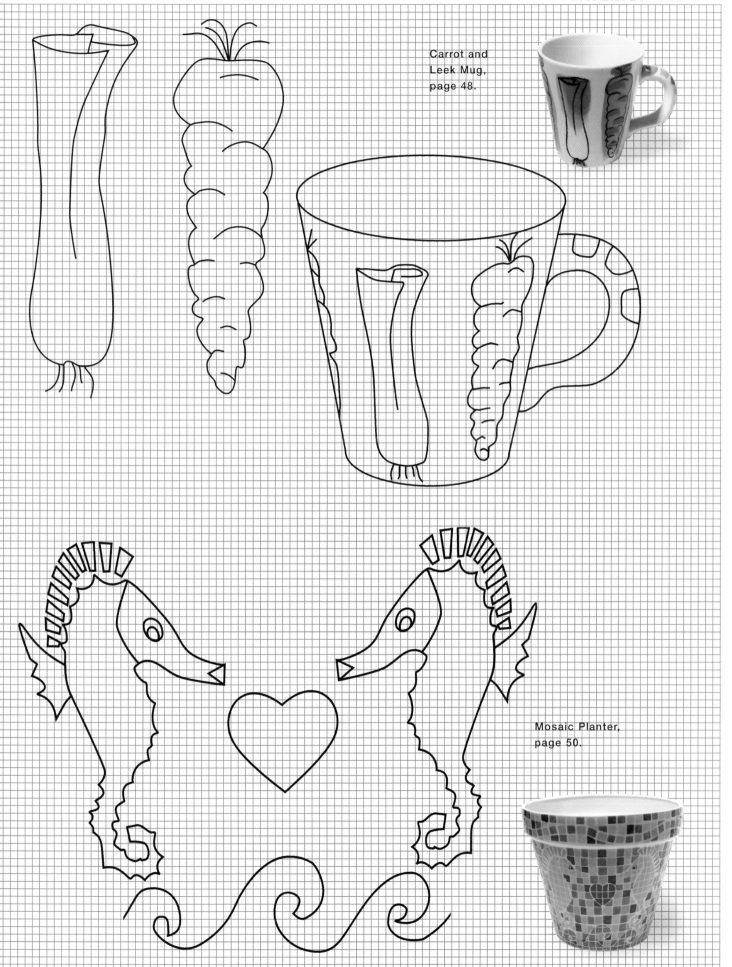

Carrot and
Leek Mug,
page 48.

Mosaic Planter,
page 50.

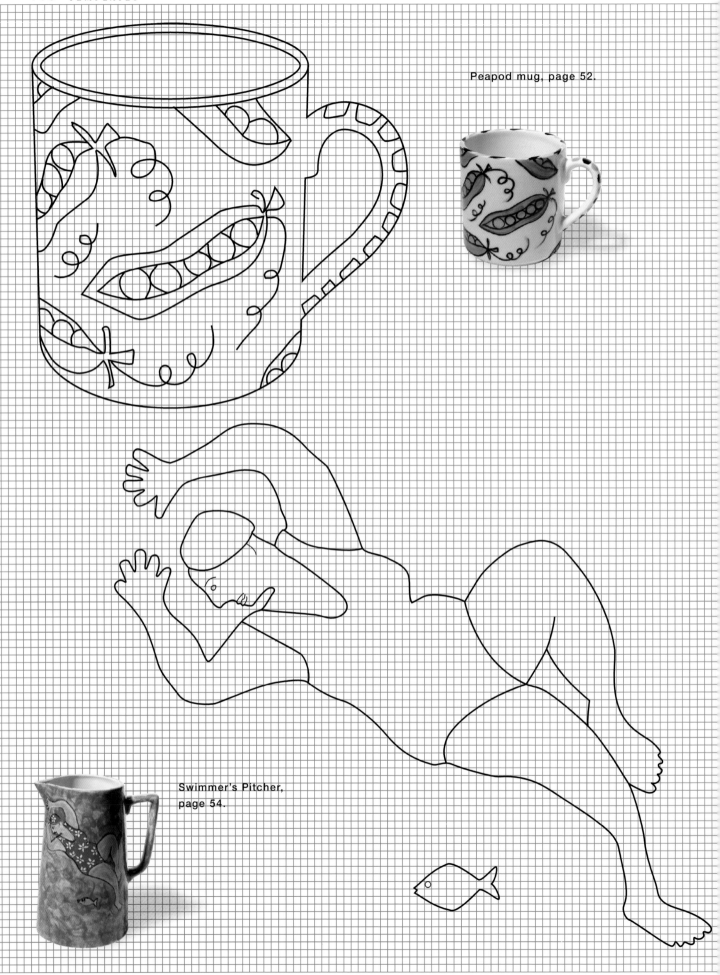

Peapod mug, page 52.

Swimmer's Pitcher,
page 54.

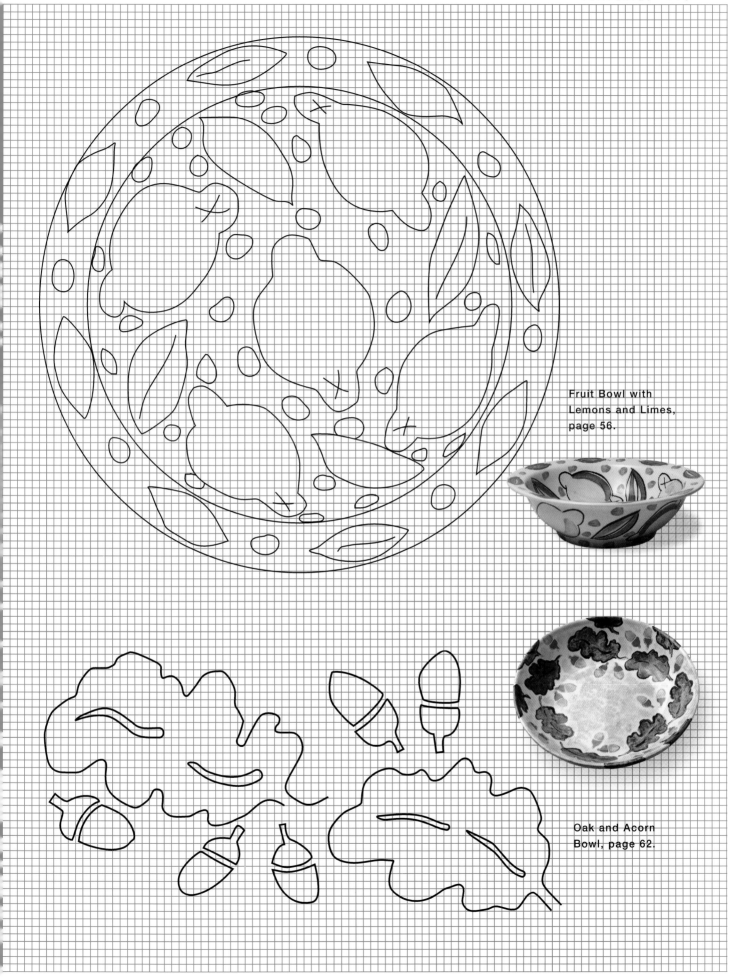

Fruit Bowl with
Lemons and Limes,
page 56.

Oak and Acorn
Bowl, page 62.

Child's Sheep Plate, page 64.

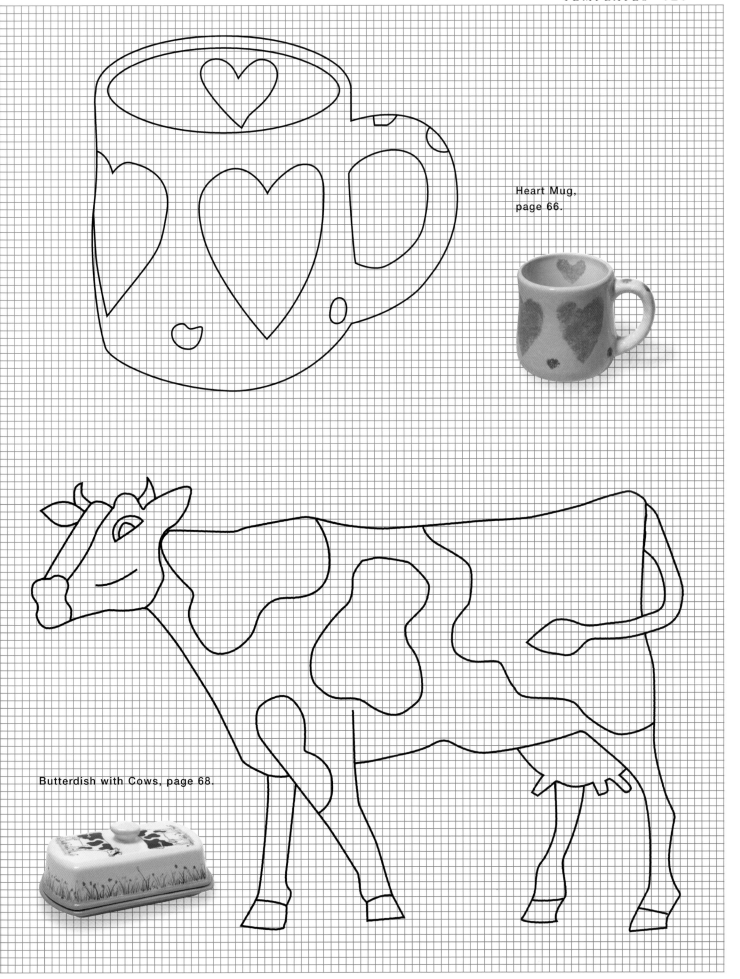

Heart Mug,
page 66.

Butterdish with Cows, page 68.

Luster Fish-motif Box
and Lid, page 78.

Rooster Pitcher, page 82.

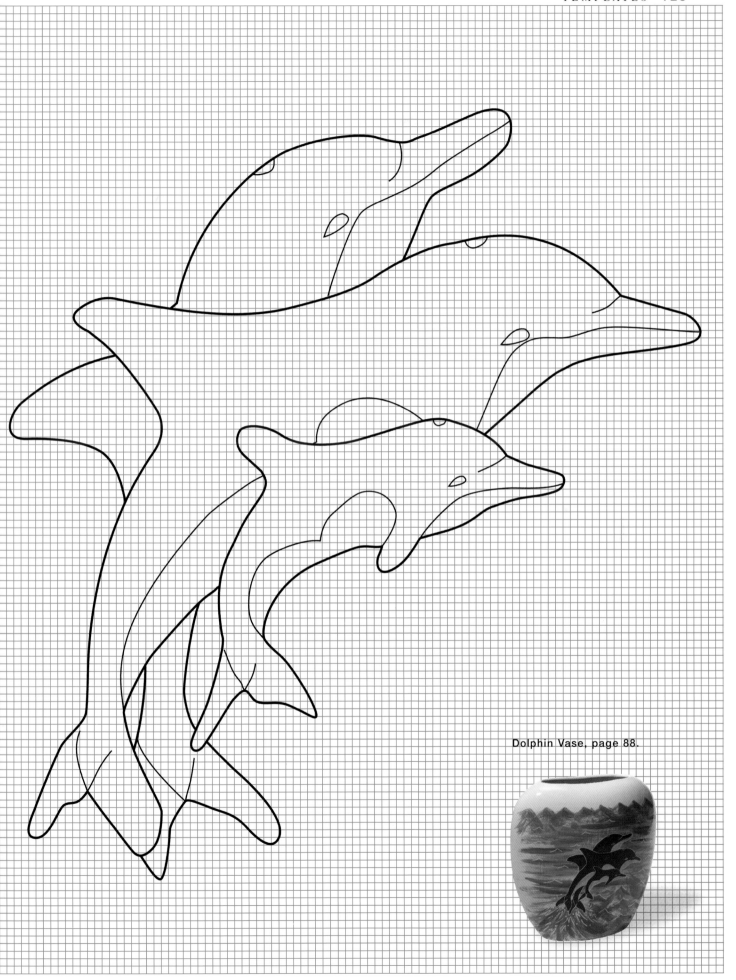

Dolphin Vase, page 88.

Aboriginal Round
Platter, page 91.

Wedding Platter, page 94.

Holly and Ivy Lamp Base, page 100.

index

QUARTO PUBLISHING PLC WOULD LIKE TO THANK THE FOLLOWING PEOPLE FOR THEIR HELP DURING THE PRODUCTION OF THIS BOOK:

SCOTT BLADES, OF THE KEW CERAMICS CAFÉ, WHERE ALL THE PAINTING DEMONSTRATIONS WERE PHOTOGRAPHED, GLAZED AND FIRED.

THE KEW CERAMICS CAFÉ IS AT 1A MORTLAKE TERRACE, MORTLAKE ROAD, KEW, SURREY TW9 3DT,

WITH A FURTHER BRANCH AT THE CERAMICS CAFÉ, 215 KING STREET, LONDON W6 9JT.

SPECIAL THANKS ARE DUE TO ALL THE ARTISTS WHO PAINTED THE PROJECTS FOR THIS BOOK:

SHARON CLARK
JOE CROUCH
SARINA DE MAJO
SILVA LEE DE MAJO BURROWS
ORNELLA GALLUCCIO
STEVEN JENKINS
SUE TAYLOR
JO WOOD
AND TO SCOTT BLADES FOR THE DEMONSTRATIONS IN THE BASIC TECHNIQUES SECTION.

UNLESS OTHERWISE STATED, ALL THE ARTISTS CAN BE CONTACTED AT THE KEW CERAMICS CAFE.

JOE CROUCH CAN BE CONTACTED AT ILLUSTRATED POTTERS, 70 CAMDEN LOCK PLACE, CHALK FARM ROAD, LONDON NW1 8AF.

ORNELLA GALLUCCIO CAN BE CONTACTED AT THE BRUSH 'N' BISQUE-IT, 77 CHURCH ROAD, BARNES, LONDON SW13 9HH, WHERE HER PROJECTS WERE ALSO GLAZED AND FIRED.

THE TILES USED AS A BACKGROUND ON PAGES 8 TO 13, AND FEATURED ON PAGE 1, WERE KINDLY SUPPLIED BY GEORGINA NOBLE AT POOH HALL, WOODSIDE, CLUN, SHROPSHIRE SY7 0JB.

FOR THE GALLERY SECTION, THE FOLLOWING ARTISTS KINDLY LOANED THEIR PERSONAL WORK:

KATE BYRNE AT POND FARM COTTAGE, HOLTON, OXFORDSHIRE OX33 1PY.

SETH CARDEW AT WENFORD BRIDGE POTTERY, ST BREWARD, BODMIN, CORNWALL PL30 3PN.

DAPHNE CARNEGY AT KINGSGATE WORKSHOPS, 110-116 KINGSGATE ROAD, LONDON NW6 2JG.

KATE GLANVILLE AT FARMERS, BETHLEHEM, CARMARTHENSHIRE SA19 9BS.

JACKIE KOHLER AT JACKAL DESIGNS, 56 WEST 22ND STREET, NEW YORK, NY 10010, USA

AND AT ORIGINE, 47 WHITE HART LANE, BARNES, LONDON SW13 0PP.

GILLES LE CORRE AT 19 HOWARD STREET, OXFORD OX4 3AY.

MIKE LEVY AT 6 VICTORIA STREET, BRIGHTON BN1 3FP.

SUE MASTERS AT CHASEFIELD, 50 PORTWAY, WELLS, SOMERSET BA5 2BW.

IAN MORRIS AND KATHRYN PHALP AT MAP, 165A JUNCTION ROAD, LONDON N19 5PZ.

LYN O'NEIL AT CHINA BEASTS, GANNETTS COTTAGE, TODBER, STURMINSTER NEWTON, DORSET DT10 1HS.

JOHN POLLEX AT WHITE LANE GALLERY, 1 WHITE LANE, BARBICAN, PLYMOUTH, DEVON PL1 2LP.

GAYNOR REEVE AT CALLIS COURT, LONDON ROAD, WEST MALLING, KENT, ME19 5AH.

SIMON THOMASON AND MARLYSE MICHEL AT THOMASON-MICHEL CERAMICS, 37 MILL ROAD, LEWES, EAST SUSSEX BN7 2RU.